NEW YORK WALKS

SEE THE CITY LIKE A LOCAL

CONTENTS

WALKS

rdia

ennedy

1000 m

THE BEST OF NEW YORK IN 6 WALKS

WALK 1 > WALL STREET & LOWER EAST SIDE p. 18
Historic Wall Street is where the city's roots lie, and on the Lower East Side you'll find many trendy boutiques and restaurants. You'll also pass through Chinatown.

WALK 2 > NOLITA, SOHO, WEST VILLAGE & HIGH LINE p. 38
This is the heart of the city. You'll find galleries and boutiques in SoHo, a bohemian vibe in the West Village, trendy shops and bars in NoLIta and the Meatpacking District, and a view from above from the High Line.

WALK 3 > TIMES SQUARE & UNION SQUARE p. 58
From Rockefeller Center and Times Square to MoMA, the Chrysler and Empire State Buildings, and Union Square, this walk takes you to some of New York City's most iconic attractions.

WALK 4 > UPPER EAST SIDE & CENTRAL PARK p. 78

Escape some of the city's bustle in the tree-lined streets of the chic Upper East Side. This walk includes all the major museums on the east side of the city, plus Central Park.

WALK 5 > UPPER WEST SIDE & HARLEM p. 98
Walk along the Hudson River through some of NYC's lesser-known recreational areas, visit Columbia University, and learn about the history of Jazz and African-American culture in Harlem.

WALK 6 > WILLIAMSBURG p. 118
Tucked in among the Brooklyn warehouses on the East River, Williamsburg is home to many of the city's artists and hipsters. You'll find amazing coffeehouses, restaurants, and secondhand shops.

NEW YORK WALKS

NEW YORK-BOUND!

The Big Apple may be known for its skyscrapers, yellow cabs, and attractions such as Times Square, the Guggenheim, the 9/11 Memorial, and Central Park, but it's the many diverse neighborhoods—each with its own distinct character and vibe—that make New York such an inspiring city. From exotic Chinatown and trendy SoHo to the nocturnal Meatpacking District and creative Williamsburg, NYC has something for everyone. Want to know the best spots to go in each part of the city? We'll show you.

WELCOME TO NEW YORK

Step off the plane and head straight for the hippest spots in town. Discover where to get the best bites in the city or grab a microbrew on tap. In *Moon New York Walks,* local authors share with you the highlights of the city they love. Stroll through New York at your own pace, taking in local hotspots on your way to the latest and greatest attractions. Savor every second of your trip.

ABOUT THIS BOOK

Moon New York Walks lets you discover the city by foot and at your own pace, so you can relax and experience the local lifestyle without having to do a lot of preparation beforehand. That means more time for you—what we call "time to momo." Our walks take you past our favorite restaurants, cafés, museums, galleries, shops, and other notable attractions—places in the city we ourselves enjoy.

None of the places mentioned here have paid to appear in either the text or photos, and all text has been written by an independent editorial staff. This is true for places in this book as well as for information in the **time to momo app** and all the latest tips, themed walks, neighborhood information, blogs, and the selection of best hotels on **www.timetomomo.com.**

CITY
NEW YORK

WORK & ACTIVITIES
CLOTHING AND INTERIOR DESIGNER

LOCAL
WENDY MAHIEU

Wendy is a passionate traveler and loves to visit the world's most beautiful places. Wherever she goes she looks for inspiration in the architecture, interior design, and art she sees. Wendy fell in love with New York and drew on the things that inspired her when putting this guide together. She'll show you a fresh, surprising side of the city that never sleeps.

PRACTICAL INFORMATION

The six walks in this book help you discover happening neighborhoods by foot and at your own pace, taking you to museums and notable attractions as well as places for great food and drinks, shopping, and entertainment. Check out the map at the front of this book to see which areas of the city the walks will take you through.

Each walk is clearly indicated on a detailed map at the beginning of each chapter. The map also specifies where each listing is located. The color of the number tells you what type of venue it is (see the key at the bottom of this page). A description of each place is given later in the chapter.

Without taking into consideration extended stops at various locations, each walk will take a maximum of three hours. The approximate distance is indicated at the top of the page, before the directions. If you want to cut a walk short, it's easy to hop on the subway (subway stops are marked on the maps with an "M").

PRICE INDICATION
We give an idea of how much you can expect to spend at each location along with its address and contact details. Unless otherwise stated, the amount given in restaurant listings is the average price of a main course. For sights and attractions, we indicate the cost of a regular full-price ticket.

NYC CONVENTIONS
New Yorkers love eating out, perhaps because the average NYC kitchen is so small. Whatever the case, there are nearly 20,000 restaurants to choose from.

LEGEND

● >> SIGHTS & ATTRACTIONS   ● >> FOOD & DRINK
● >> SHOPPING   ● >> MORE TO EXPLORE

Most New Yorkers go out for dinner between 7pm and 9pm. Reservations often aren't necessary, except at particularly classic or trendy restaurants, where you may have to book far in advance or be ready to wait. When in doubt, call ahead or make reservations online at *www.OpenTable.com.*

When you get your bill, you'll notice the sales tax has been added. There is an 8.875% tax on all restaurant meals in New York. Since a tip of 15-20 percent is expected, a handy rule of thumb for those who don't want to bother with the math is to simply double the amount charged for sales tax and leave that as a tip. Always tip your servers and bartenders, regardless of the quality of service— they rely on tips as part of their income. Be aware that if you are with a group of five or more, a 20 percent gratuity is automatically added to the bill in some restaurants. Always read the fine print on the menu and check your bill closely before you pay to make sure you don't tip twice.

Sales tax on clothes and shoes is roughly 4.5 percent, and this generally is not included in the price tag. For other products, such as cosmetics and household items, the sales tax is 8.8 percent. The tax for hotel rooms is 14.75 percent.

FESTIVALS AND EVENTS

Something's always going on in New York. Notable events include:

Usually in February > Lunar New Year Parade
March 17 > St. Patrick's Day Parade
Late June > Coney Island Mermaid Parade
Last weekend in June > NYC Pride March
Second Sunday in June > Puerto Rican Day Parade
October 31 > Village Halloween Parade
Early November > New York City Marathon
Fourth Thursday in November > Macy's Thanksgiving Day Parade
Late November-late December > Christmas in Rockefeller Center
December 31 > New Year's Eve in Times Square

HAVE ANY TIPS?

Shops and restaurants in New York come and go fairly regularly. We do our best to keep the walks and contact details as up to date as possible, and this is immediately reflected in our digital products. We update the print edition as often as we can. If, despite our best efforts, you can't find a certain place or if you have any other comments or tips about this book, please email info@momedia.nl or leave a message at **www.timetomomo.com.**

TUNED IN TO NEW YORK!

GO TO WWW.TIMETOMOMO.COM FOR THE LATEST TIPS
NEW ADDRESSES + UP-AND-COMING NEIGHBORHOODS
+ POP-UP STORES + CONCERTS + FESTIVALS + MUCH MORE

TRANSPORTATION

The most direct way to get to and from the airport is by taxi. A trip from **John F. Kennedy (JFK) Airport** to Manhattan will take you between 40 minutes to an hour, depending on traffic, for a set rate of $52.50 (plus toll). Rides from JFK to other parts of the city will cost you $38-65. The journey from **Newark,** New Jersey to the city will also take 40-60 minutes, and the ride will cost $50-75 (plus toll). From Manhattan heading back to Newark Airport, you'll have to pay what's on the meter, plus an additional $17.50. If you're flying into **LaGuardia** in Queens, the ride to Manhattan will take 20-40 minutes and cost $20-35. Don't forget to factor in a tip; it's customary to tip taxi drivers 15-20 percent. The ride-sharing app Lyft also services NYC-area airports.

A less-expensive alternative is to take a **shuttle,** such as New York Airport Service Express *(www.nyairportservice.com)*, Olympia Airport Express *(www.olympiabus.com)*, or SuperShuttle *(www.supershuttle.com)*. Shuttles cost $12-23 per person.

It's also possible to get from the airport into the city using public transportation. **Bus** M60 from LaGuardia brings you to Manhattan. From Newark, the AirTrain will get you to Penn Station in Midtown in 45 minutes for $12. And from JFK, the AirTrain delivers you to the E train, which you can take into the city.

Once you're in the city, the fastest way to get around is by **subway.** It's generally clean and safe, provided that you don't flaunt all your valuables. To use the subway you'll need a MetroCard. These are available in SingleRide tickets ($3), Pay-Per-Ride cards, or Unlimited Ride cards for specific durations of time. Pay-per-ride cards work with a balance ($80 maximum), and you'll get bonus credit when you put $10 or more on your card. The Unlimited Ride cards come in two options: 7-day unlimited rides ($31) or 30-day unlimited rides ($116.50). You can use your card as much as you want during this period, but only once every 18 minutes and for one person at a time.

Subways stops are often named, simply enough, after the street where they're located. Some stations have convenient separate entrances for trains heading

north (uptown) and those heading south (downtown). At every station you'll find a map of the subway and any special service notices, which are also available at *www.mta.info*.

There are plenty of **taxis** in NYC. Just stick your hand out and one will soon stop for you. Taxis are available when the number on top is illuminated. When the words "off duty" are lit up, the driver isn't picking up customers, and when no light is on, the taxi is occupied. When telling the driver where you want to go, it's handy if you also know the cross streets (for example, 52nd Street, between 1st and 2nd).

Taxis can carry a maximum of four passengers, and the average price for a three-mile ride is $7-11, depending on the traffic and time of day. For shorter journeys, tip about $1-2; for longer rides tip around 15-20 percent. You can pay for a cab in cash or with a credit card. When you pay with a card, the machine will suggest a tip for you. Always ask for a receipt before you leave the cab. It has the taxi number on it, which is convenient if there is a problem or you accidentally leave something behind.

BIKING

Bikes have become an increasingly popular way to explore New York City. Since the city continues to create new bike lanes, you'll see more and more New Yorkers hopping on the saddle too. Traffic may be chaotic, but biking is a trend that's here to stay. The most popular bike routes are through Central Park, over the Brooklyn Bridge, along the Brooklyn Esplanade, next to the Hudson River, and through the eastern part of Manhattan.

Citi Bike *(www.citibikenyc.com)* is NYC's bike share program, which anyone can use. There are hundreds of stations across the city where you can rent a bike. After you're done, simply return it to any station for the next person to use. Bikes are available in 30-minute increments, which can be extended to 60 minutes for an additional fee. You can also opt for a day pass ($12) or week pass ($25). For long journeys, it may be a better idea to rent a bicycle through a bike shop, which will cost about $8-10 for two hours. If you choose to go this route, it's a good idea to reserve your bike or tour online, particularly during high season. Reservations can be made online via *www.bikenewyorkcity.com.*

Need a break from the city that never sleeps? Take a **bike ride** along the Hudson River. Start in the West Village at the Waterfront Bicycle Shop *(www.bikeshopny.com)* or book a tour through Rolling Orange Bike Tours *(www.rollingorangebikes.com).*

New York City traffic can be particularly hectic. Bike lanes are usually on the left-hand side of the road, but sometimes continue on the opposite side of the street. Not all drivers are accustomed to the significant increase in two-wheel traffic, so always remain alert and don't forget to rent a helmet with your bike if it doesn't come with one. The most important traffic rules to remember are that pedestrians have the right of way, riding on the sidewalk is not allowed, cyclists must ride in the same direction as traffic, and traffic lights and signs apply to bikes the same way as they do to cars. Traffic rules are strictly enforced and the fines for breaking them are hefty.

Visit *www.nycgo.com/articles/bike-itineraries* for more information about cycling in New York City.

1 Enjoy amazing Italian at **Bar Primi.** > 325 Bowery

2 Dine at Michelin-star **The Musket Room.** > 265 Elizabeth Street

3 **Malaparte** has delicious Italian food. > 753 Washington Street

4 **The Fat Radish** serves up healthy fare in a former factory. > p. 29

5 **Public** is the perfect spot for an intimate dinner. > p. 46

6 **East Pole** is a wonderful option for a sumptuous lunch. > p. 90

7 Enjoy the friendly atmosphere and authentic tacos at **Tacombi.** > p.45

8 Savor delicious food and wine at **Aria Wine Bar.** > p. 49

9 Meat lovers won't want to miss **Fette Sau** in Williamsburg. > p. 125

10 Get amazingly fresh seafood at **Mary's Fish Camp.** > p. 49

TOP 10 | ART & CULTURE

1   **Le Bain** is an extravagant rooftop bar with a pool. > p. 49

2   Authentic beer garden **Radegast Hall & Biergarten.** > 113 N 3rd Street, Brooklyn

3   The biggest rooftop bar: **Press Lounge.** > 653 11th Avenue

4   Speakeasy-style bar **Angel's Share.** > 8 Stuyvesant Street

5   The best jazz in the city at **Smalls Jazz Club.** > 183 W 10th Street

6   Head to **Comedy Cellar** for stand-up. > 117 Macdougal Street

7   **Ear Inn** is an old sailors' bar. > 326 Spring Street

8   Pool, jazz, and inexpensive beer at **Fat Cat.** > 75 Christopher Street

9   Vintage video games + beer = **Barcade.** > 388 Union Ave

10   **Lillie's** is an extravagant Victorian bar with live music. > 249 W 49th Street

TOP 10 | COFFEE

1 Enjoy coffee in **Double Dutch Espresso**'s garden. > p. 113

2 Australian **Toby's Estate** serves delicious coffee. > p. 126

3 Relax with a window side drink at **El Rey.** > p. 30

4 Grab your coffee on the go at **Saturdays Surf.** > p. 53

5 **Maman** for coffee and chocolate cookies. > 239 Centre Street

6 **Stumptown Coffee Roasters** in the hip Ace hotel. > p. 72

7 **Little Collins** has the best espresso in town. > p. 70

8 Stop for coffee in **Bakeri**'s inviting backyard garden. > p. 126

9 **Homecoming** is located in NYC's hippest neighborhood. > p. 141

10 **Happy Bones** coffee is famous on Instagram. > 394 Broome Street

WALK 1

WALL STREET & LOWER EAST SIDE

ABOUT THE WALK

This walk takes you down historic Wall Street, where the roots of the city and capitalism lie. You'll also get to explore the Lower East Side, where young, creative professionals haunt trendy shops and popular restaurants. Finally, the walk will take you to Chinatown, a neighborhood that has recently attracted many of the city's young residents thanks to lower rent. And, of course, Chinatown is great for the amazing food you can get without breaking the bank.

THE NEIGHBORHOODS

Up until the 19th century, life in New York City was primarily concentrated in a small part of what is now Lower Manhattan. Around 1700, the city extended slightly beyond Fulton Street, and 100 years later only a handful of additional apartment blocks had been built. When **City Hall** opened in 1812, it seemed unimaginable that the city would continue growing to the north. This historic area is rich with beautiful buildings dating back to some of the city's earliest days, from the imposing Gregorian and Federal-style architecture around **Wall Street** to the apartment buildings and temples in **Chinatown.**

Bustling Chinatown was once a dangerous neighborhood. At the end of the 19th century, it was often the scene of fighting between street gangs like the Dead Rabbits and Bowery Boys. Apartments in what is today Columbus Park were infamous, and places there gained notorious nicknames such as Bone Alley, Kerosene Row, and Bandits' Roost. Today's Chinatown has long since shaken off this negative reputation. The dynamic neighborhood is now a popular destination for many young New Yorkers thanks to a plethora of shops and restaurants.

The **Lower East Side** is one of the oldest neighborhoods in the city. Some 200 years ago this area was flooded with immigrants, and the **Lower East Side Tenement Museum** in Orchard Street is an excellent place to learn about how

they lived and to gain insight into the history of the neighborhood. Today the area is becoming increasingly more gentrified and many young people are attracted to the trendy bars, cafés, and boutiques. With its numerous galleries, the neighborhood also appeals to art aficionados. Look up from time to time while walking around. This neighborhood is full of beautiful brick buildings with those great fire escapes that are so characteristic of New York City.

SHORT ON TIME? HERE ARE THE HIGHLIGHTS
+ STATEN ISLAND FERRY + CENTURY 21 + 9/11 MEMORIAL / TRIBUTE CENTER + BROOKLYN BRIDGE + SCHILLER'S LIQUOR BAR

TIPS
// During the week is the best time to explore historic Wall Street
// Visit the Lower East Side at the end of the day or on the weekend
// The last part of the walk is perfect for biking

WALL STREET & LOWER EAST SIDE

1. Staten Island Ferry
2. Castle Clinton
3. Netherlands Monument
4. National Museum of the American Indian
5. Fraunces Tavern
6. Stone Street
7. Federal Hall National Memorial
8. New York Stock Exchange
9. Trinity Church
10. 9/11 Memorial/Tribute Center
11. Century 21
12. St. Paul's Chapel
13. 9/11 Memorial Museum
14. Woolworth Building
15. City Hall
16. Brooklyn Bridge
17. Municipal Building
18. CityStore
19. Columbus Park
20. Chinatown
21. The Fat Radish
22. The Leadbelly
23. Dimes
24. Hester Street Fair
25. Dudley's
26. Catinca Tabacaru Gallery
27. Top Hat
28. Castle Fitzjohns Gallery
29. Lower East Side Tenement Museum
30. El Rey
31. Frankie
32. Rachel Uffner
33. Schiller's Liquor Bar
34. Edith Machinist

WALK 1 DESCRIPTION (approx. 4.6 miles)

From Staten Island Ferry terminal ❶, go left into Battery Park and then walk right along the water to visit the castle and the Netherlands Monument ❷ ❸. On the other side of the park, check out the National Museum of the American Indian ❹. Then turn right on Whitehall Street and left on Bridge Street. Visit Fraunces Tavern ❺ on the corner across the street and to the right, then head straight down Pearl Street. At the end of the block, turn left and then right on Stone Street for breakfast ❻. Turn left on William Street, and left again on Wall Street for more sightseeing ❼ ❽ ❾. When you come out of Trinity Church, turn left and then left again on Thames Street. Continue straight to Greenwich Street for a visit to the 9/11 Memorial ❿. Turn right, then right again on Liberty Street. Turn left on Church Street and snag some good deals on designer clothes ⓫. Then take a right to visit St. Paul's Chapel ⓬. On Vesey Street ⓭ turn right toward Broadway. Then make a left and walk past the Woolworth Building ⓮. Cross the street and walk through the park near City Hall ⓯ toward the Brooklyn Bridge ⓰, the Municipal Building ⓱, and a souvenir shop ⓲. Continue on Centre Street to Worth Street and turn right. Walk through Columbus Park ⓳ and exit at Mulberry Street. Turn right, then left on Mosco Street. Make a left on Mott Street toward Chinatown ⓴. Go right on Bayard Street, then left on Elizabeth Street. Continue straight until Hester Street, then turn right and head toward the Lower East Side. Take a right on Allen Street and a left on Canal Street. There are lots of nice spots for lunch here on this street or left down Orchard Street ㉑ ㉒ ㉓. Turn left on Essex Street—you may catch the weekly market ㉔. Next, make a left on Hester Street and right on Orchard Street ㉕. Turn right on Broome Street to see some art and do some shopping ㉖ ㉗. Head down Orchard Street for some famous works of art ㉘ and the Tenement Museum ㉙. Continue down Orchard Street and then turn right on Stanton Street ㉚ ㉛. There is more art to be seen to the left on Suffolk Street ㉜. Then take a right on Suffolk Street and finish off with a glass of wine to the right on Rivington Street ㉝, or score a nice vintage item ㉞.

SIGHTS & ATTRACTIONS

② **Castle Clinton** was built in 1811 on a manmade island to protect the harbor from the British. Later, it functioned as a theater and then as a landing depot; between 1855 and 1890, some eight million immigrants passed through here. For a while the castle was even home to the New York Aquarium. Today, you can purchase tickets here for the ferry to the Statue of Liberty and Ellis Island.
battery park, www.nps.gov/cacl, t: (212) 344-7220, open daily 7:45am-5pm, free entrance, 1 train to south ferry, 4 & 5 trains to bowling green

③ In 1926, 300 years after the establishment of New Amsterdam, the Dutch government presented a flagstaff to the city of New York. The **Netherlands Monument** is now a daily reminder that New York City once began as a Dutch trading post. Images on the pedestal depict how the Dutch "purchased" the island of Manhattan from the Native Americans.
battery park, 1 train to south ferry, 4 & 5 trains to bowling green

④ On the site where Fort Amsterdam stood during the 17th century now stands the U.S. Custom House. The custom house was completed in 1907, at a time when the Port of New York was the most important port in the United States. Sixty percent of all customs duties in the country were collected here. Now the first three stories of the building house the **National Museum of the American Indian,** which has permanent and temporary exhibitions about the Native peoples of the Americas.
1 bowling green, www.nmai.si.edu, t: (212) 514-3700, open mon-wed & fri-sun 10am-5pm, thu 10am-8pm, free entrance, 4 & 5 trains to bowling green, 1 train to south ferry

⑦ **Federal Hall National Memorial** stands on the site where George Washington took the oath of office as the first U.S. president and where the first Congress convened. The current building was previously a U.S. custom house and once contained over $300 million in silver and gold. Today, it houses a museum about Washington's inauguration, freedom of the press, and the Federal Hall (the first capitol), which once stood on this spot.
26 wall street, at broad street, www.nps.gov/feha, t: (212) 825-6990, open mon-fri 9am-5pm, free entrance, 2 & 3 trains to wall st

⑧ The **New York Stock Exchange** dates back to 1792, when 24 brokers agreed to deal only with each other and to set a fixed commission rate. Share trading began in 1865. The main building of the current exchange, located on Broad Street, is the most imposing, with its large columns and enormous flag. The building opened in 1903 and had air-conditioning even then. The building has been closed to the public since 9/11.

11 wall street, www.nyse.com, t: (212) 864-7752, 2 & 3 trains to wall st

⑨ **Trinity Church** is a beautiful example of Neo-Gothic architecture, and a few of the earliest Dutch colonists are buried in the cemetery here.

74 trinity place, broadway entrance, www.trinitywallstreet.org t: (212) 602-0800, open mon-fri 7am-6pm, sat 8am-4pm, sun 7am-4pm, sun service 9am & 11:15am, free entrance, 2, 3, 4 & 5 trains to wall st, 1, n & r trains to rector st, j, m & z trains to broad st

⑩ The **9/11 Memorial,** which stands on the site where the World Trade Center once stood, is an incredibly moving spot commemorating the victims of the 9/11 attacks. Victims' names are inscribed on parapets surrounding two reflecting pools located in the footprints of the Twin Towers. You can reserve your tickets in advance at *www.911memorial.org*. Be sure to also visit the **9/11 Tribute Center,** located at 120 Liberty Street, to see exhibits of victims' personal objects and take a tour with someone directly affected by the attacks.

corner of albany and greenwich street, www.tributewtc.org, t: (212) 266-5211, memorial open daily 7:30am-9pm, tribute center open mon-sat 9am-6pm, sun 10am-5pm, free entrance to 9/11 memorial, visitors entrance c, e train to world trade center, a, c, j, z, 2, 3, 4 & 5 trains to fulton street

⑫ **St. Paul's Chapel** has miraculously survived the Revolutionary War and two terrorist attacks on the World Trade Center relatively unscathed. In the hours, weeks, and months that followed 9/11, the chapel was where rescue and recovery workers from Ground Zero received care and support. Visitors can see photos and read stories from this time inside the chapel.

209 broadway, www.trinitywallstreet.org, t: (212) 602-0800, open mon-sat 10am-6pm, sun 7am-6pm, sun service 8am, 9:15am & 8pm, free entrance, 2, 3, 4, 5, a & c trains to broadway-nassau st

⑬ Take the time to visit the **9/11 Memorial Museum,** where you can check out an exhibition that presents the attack on the World Trade Center in three parts: the events of the day itself, the history leading up to that day, and the impact after the attack. The museum regularly organizes films and talks.

20 vesey street, www.911memorial.org/museum, t: (212) 266-5211, open sun-thu 9am-8pm, fri-sat 9am-9pm, entrance $24, a, c, j, z, 2, 3, 4 & 5 trains to fulton st, e train to world trade center

⑭ Construction of the **Woolworth Building** cost $13.5 million back in 1913. It was the tallest building in the world until 1930, and the observation deck on the 58th floor was a popular tourist attraction until 1945. The building is Neo-Gothic in style and characterized by spires, gargoyles, flying buttresses, and vaulted ceilings.

233 park place, at barclay street, not open to the public, 2 & 3 trains to park place

⑮ **City Hall** houses the offices of the mayor and city council, among others. A small collection of memorabilia is on display in the building, and free tours are given during the week. Make a reservation on the website.

broadway, at chambers street, www.nyc.gov, t: (212) 639-9675, open mon-fri 9am-5pm, free entrance, 4, 5 & 6 trains to brooklyn bridge-city hall, r train to city hall

⑰ The awe-inspiring **Municipal Building** was built in 1909 to create additional office space for municipal agencies. The building is capped by the copper statue *Civic Fame,* a female figure holding a five-pointed crown symbolizing the five boroughs of the city.

1 centre street, open mon-fri 9am-5:30pm, free entrance, 4, 5 & 6 trains to brooklyn bridge-city hall, r train to city hall

㉙ Discover what life was like for millions of New York immigrants in the late 19th and early 20th centuries at the **Lower East Side Tenement Museum.** To visit the museum, you must sign up for a tour. Making reservations in advance is recommended.

103 orchard street, www.tenement.org, t: (212) 975-3786, open daily 10am-6:30pm, thu 10am-8:30pm, entrance $25, f, j, m & z trains to delancey st/essex st

FOOD & DRINK

(5) **Fraunces Tavern** is more than just a bar and restaurant—it's also a museum where you can learn about the Revolutionary War. Founding Father George Washington and his officers celebrated their victory here with a festive dinner.

54 pearl street, at broad street, www.frauncestavern.com, t: (212) 968-1776, open daily 11am-10pm (bar open late), price $24, r & 1 trains to whitehall st/south ferry, 2 & 3 trains to wall st

(7) **Stone Street** gets its name from the fact it was the first paved road in the city. Today, many restaurants fill the 10th century buildings, and the street's become a popular spot among Wall Street workers. When the weather is nice, the restaurants set up wooden tables in the middle of the street. For delicious breakfast and coffee, head to French bakery Financier.

stone street, between broad street and hanover street square, 2 & 3 trains to wall st, r train to whitehall st

(21) **The Fat Radish,** featuring a menu of simple, healthy dishes, is located in a former sausage factory at the edge of Chinatown and the Lower East Side. Some of the building's history is still perceptible thanks to the restaurant's industrial interior, with its high ceilings and brick walls.

17 orchard street, www.thefatradishnyc.com, t: (212) 300-4053, open tue-fri noon-3:30pm & 5:30pm-midnight, sat 11am-3:30pm & 5:30pm-midnight, sun 11am-3:30pm & 5:30pm-10pm, price $23, b & d trains to grand st, f train to east broadway

(22) Go to **The Leadbelly** for the oysters, cocktails, and music. This dark bar has live music Wednesday through Saturday during happy hour, and a DJ takes over as the evening progresses. There are plenty of yummy snacks on offer in addition to oysters. Hankering for something more filling? Head down the street to the bar's sister restaurant, The Fat Radish (#21).

14b orchard street, www.theleadbellynyc.com, t: (646) 596-9142, open mon-sat 5:30pm-2am, price $13, b & d trains to grand st, f train to east broadway

(23) You'll find **Dimes** tucked between several Chinese stores. This small spot is great for breakfast, lunch, or dinner. It serves up seasonal dishes, which makes

it a popular place among the city's health-conscious, and the clean, light interior will put you in a good mood. In addition to to serving food, Dimes also has an indoor market area where you can shop for natural cosmetics, homegoods, and quirky items, including pottery and edible fragrances.

49 canal street, www.dimesnyc.com, t: (212) 925-1300, open mon-thu 8am-11pm, fri 8am-midnight, sat 9am-11pm, sun 9am-10:30pm, price $12, f train to east broadway, j & m trains to essex st

㉕ The atmosphere in **Dudley's** is warm and inviting. This charming corner restaurant is always busy; local residents often stop here for a bite on their way to or from work. Have a cocktail at the bar or sit at the window for some good people watching. The classic American fare served here is simple but delicious. Try the Bronte-Burger.

85 orchard street, www.dudleysnyc.com, t: (212) 925-7355, open daily 9am-1am, price $20, b & d trains to grand st, f train to delancey st

㉚ After a long walk, the fresh, white interior of **El Rey** coffee bar and luncheonette is a perfect place to sit and relax. Order something to drink and sit at the window, where you can watch the locals as they come and go. The small menu offers a nice selection of healthy options.

100 stanton street, www.elreynyc.com, t: (212) 260-3950, open mon-fri 7am-10:30pm, sat-sun 8am-10:30pm, price $9, j, m & z trains to essex st

㉝ **Schiller's Liquor Bar** is a casual neighborhood restaurant with simple dishes and a wine list that divides its offerings into three catagories: cheap, decent, and good—although according to Schiller, cheap is also really good!

131 rivington street, www.schillersny.com, t: (212) 260-4555, open mon-thu 11am-1am, fri 11am-3am, sat 10am-3am, sun 10am-5pm, price $20, f train to delancey st, j, m & z trains to essex st, b & d trains to grand st

SHOPPING

⑪ **Century 21:** Where bargain hunters' dreams come true. At this department store's flagship, you'll find racks of brand-name designer clothes at significantly

24

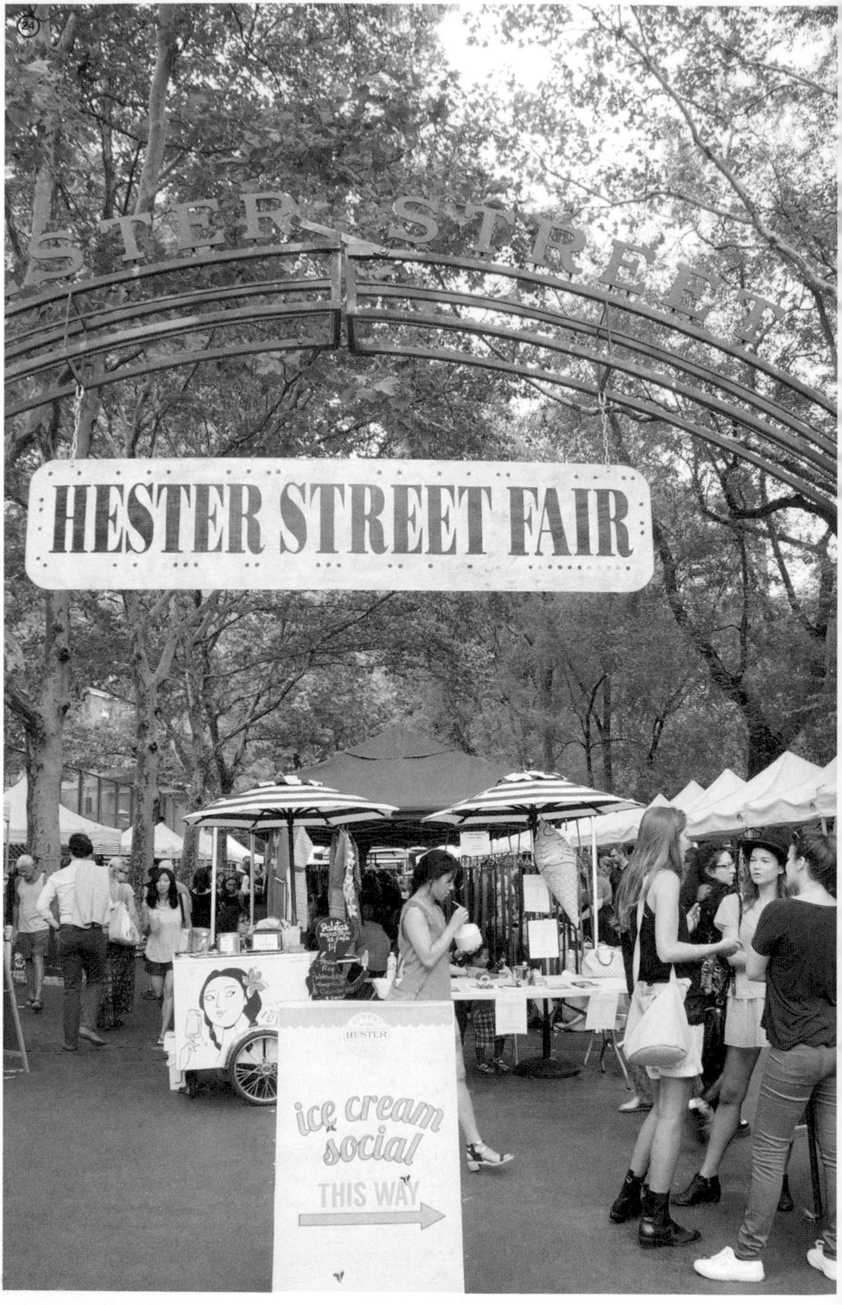

discounted prices. The store is so big it may take a while before you make it to the department you came in for.

22 cortlandt street, www.c21stores.com, t: (212) 227-9092, open mon-wed 7:45am-9pm, thu-fri 7:45am-9:30pm, sat 10am-9pm, sun 11am-8pm, n & r trains to cortlandt st, 4 & 5 trains to fulton st, e train to world trade center

⑱ **CityStore** is the official souvenir shop of New York City. Here you can buy subway tiles, authentic taxi medallions, and official NYPD and NYFD merchandise. Their other location is at the Manhattan Marriage Bureau, at 141 Worth Street, just a few blocks away. It offers bride and groom accessories, bridal party gifts, fresh flowers, and I Got Married in NYC merchandise.

1 centre street, north plaza, www.nyc.gov/citystore, t: (212) 386-0007, open mon-fri 10am-5pm, 4, 5, 6, j & m trains to brooklyn bridge, 1, 2, a, c & e trains to chambers st, r train to city hall

㉔ For beautiful antiques, vintage items, and a variety of other trinkets, head to **Hester Street Fair.** You'll also find lots of food vendors there, many of which offer samples. This small market always attracts big crowds.

at the corner of hester and essex street, www.hesterstreetfair.com, t: (917) 267-9496, open late april-late oct sat 11am-6pm, f train to east broadway or delancey st, f, j, m & z to essex st

㉗ The minimalist **Top Hat** offers a mix of stationery items and related products like notebooks, stamps, leather pencil cases, and bags. It also sells unique home decor and lifestyle products.

245 broome street, www.tophatnyc.com, t: (212) 677-4240, open daily noon-8pm, f train to delancey st, j, m & z trains to essex st

㉛ For a long time, this spot was home to the cool concept store Pixie Market. Now, however, the owners run **Frankie,** a shop geared toward fashion-conscious women with distinctive tastes. The shop offers a changing collection of London and Scandinavian-style clothing and accessories—including shoes, jewelry, and bags—from indie designers with an edgy aesthetic.

100 stanton street, www.thefrankieshop.com, t: (212) 253-0953, open mon-sat noon-8pm, sun noon-7pm, f train to 2nd avenue

㉞ **Edith Machinist** is an enormous vintage store full of shoes and bags from well-known and obscure brands alike. Prices may be on the higher end, but you can rest assured you're getting something unique. See something in the store you're sorry you passed up? Don't sweat it, you can continue shopping online.
104 rivington street, www.edithmachinist.com, t: (212) 979-9992, open mon, fri, sun noon-6pm, tue-thu & sat noon-7pm, f train to delancey, j, m & z trains to essex st

MORE TO EXPLORE

① A ride on the **Staten Island Ferry** is a fun and free way to see the Statue of Liberty and the New York City skyline. Aside from the occasional savvy tourist, the ferry is primarily used by commuters from Staten Island. Altogether, a trip to Staten Island and back takes about an hour, and you never have to wait too long for the next boat.
whitehall terminal, www.siferry.com, t: (718) 815-2628, runs daily 24 hours, free, 1 train to south ferry, 4 & 5 trains to bowling green, n & r trains to whitehall st

⑯ Construction of the 5,989-foot long **Brooklyn Bridge** began in 1870 and was completed 13 years later. The Gothic granite towers and steel cables are now an iconic New York City landmark. Walk across the bridge for an amazing view of both Manhattan and Brooklyn, which is particularly beautiful at sunset.
park row, near centre street, 4, 5 & 6 trains to brooklyn bridge-city hall, n & r trains to city hall

⑲ **Columbus Park** is located in what was once one of the worst neighborhoods in the city. Today, however, the park is a peaceful backdrop to scenes of women chatting over games of cards, men hunkering over Chinese chess boards, and children playing and having fun. There is always lots of activity here.
mulberry street, between bayard and worth street, www.nycgovparks.org, open daily, a, c, e, j, m, n, q, r, z & 6 trains to canal st

⑳ **Chinatown** was once a dangerous neighborhood, and around the year 1900, deadly clashes between rival *tongs,* or gangs, on Doyers Street earned a bend in the road the nickname "Bloody Angle." Today, however, Chinatown is a bustling

area where there's always a lot going on. The area is full of history, which is reflected in the Kimlau Memorial, the statue of Confucius, and the Church of the Transfiguration, a church for immigrants. Enjoy delicious Chinese dumplings at the Vegetarian Dim Sum House at 24 Pell Street.

mott street, www.explorechinatown.com, j, m, n, q, r, z & 6 trains to canal st

㉖ The contemporary art on display at **Catinca Tabacaru Gallery** changes from month to month, and features conceptual works by young artists from both the U.S. and abroad. It publishes catalogues several times a year about upcoming art fairs and cultural projects to keep an eye out for.

250 broome street, www.tincaart.com, t: (212) 260-2481, open wed-sun 11am-6pm, f train to delancey st, j, m & z trains to essex st

㉘ At **Castle Fitzjohns Gallery** you'll see famous works by Andy Warhol and Roy Lichtenstein, as well as lesser-known pieces from talented young artists. The gallery always has multiple ongoing exhibitions. Owner Vincent is very active in the neighborhood and has mapped out a gallery route.

98 orchard street, www.castlefitzjohns.com, t: (212) 260-2460, open daily noon-7pm, f train to delancey st, j, m & z trains to essex st

㉜ Many talented young artists selected from around the world hold their first solo exhibitions at **Rachel Uffner.** The mostly abstract art is displayed in an amazingly light space.

170 suffolk street, www.racheluffnergallery.com, t: (212) 274-0064, open wed-sun 10am-6pm, f train to delancey st, m train to 2nd ave, j, m & z trains to essex st

WALK 2

NOLITA, SOHO, WEST VILLAGE & HIGH LINE

ABOUT THE WALK

On this walk you'll see several charming downtown neighborhoods. Discover designer boutiques and popular restaurants in NoLIta, SoHo, and the Meatpacking District. Enjoy tree-lined streets and admire beautiful 18th- and 19th-century architecture in the romantic West Village.

THE NEIGHBORHOODS

Downtown neighborhoods, south of 14th Street, feel atmospheres away from their uptown counterparts, with rambling streets that go off the grid.

Trendy **NoLIta** (short for "North of Little Italy") is an area located between East Houston, the Bowery, Broome Street, and Lafayette Street. Elizabeth Street in particular is well-known for its lovely shops and boutiques. NoLIta is such a small neighborhood that you'll walk right through it and into SoHo before you know it.

SoHo (short for "South of Houston Street") was originally an industrial area full of factories and warehouses, and was later taken over by artists. Today, it's a major trendsetter in the fashion world. With its grand cast-iron warehouses, luxury boutiques, fashion houses, and art galleries, it offers some of the best shopping in the city.

The **West Village** is often called "Little Bohemia," and today is home to many celebrities as well as charming shops and restaurants. Bordering it is the trendy Meatpacking District. Up until recently, this was a place where animal carcasses hung in the streets during the day, and in the 1980s the neighborhood was a hotspot for drugs and prostitution. Today, however, the district is full of high-end stores and trendy restaurants, and it's a great place for nightlife—especially if you want to do some star-spotting.

0   250 m

MIDTOWN
(CENTRAL PARK,
TIMES SQUARE &
UNION SQUARE)

23rd St
28th St

Madison
Square
Park

WALK 3

23rd St

23rd St

Rubin Mus. of Art

18th St

14th St-8th Av

14th St

14th St-
6th Av

14th St

Union
Square
Park

14th St-Union Sq

14th St-Union Sq

3rd Av

Stuyvesant
Square

FINISH

31
32

30

29

28

GANSEVOORT STREET

HORATIO STREET

JANE STREET

WEST 12TH STREET

BETHUNE STREET

BANK STREET

WEST 11TH STREET

27

26

25

24

22 23
   19
21
20

Christopher St-
Sheridan Sq

Christopher St

WALK 2

West 4th St-
Washington Sq

Washington
Square
Park

Astor Pl

8th St-NYU

17 18

Houston St

16

Mus. of
African Art

Bleecker St

Broadway-Lafayette St

1

2   START

3

4   2nd Av-Lower
      East Side

5

6   New Museum

Spring St

14

13   Prince St

15

12   10

11

Spring St

7

8

9   Bowery

Canal St

Canal St

Canal St

Canal St

Grand St

WEST
VILLAGE

Hudson River

HUDSON RIVER GREENWAY

HOLLAND TUNNEL

SOHO, NOLITA &
TRIBECA

EAST
VILLAGE &
LOWER
EAST SIDE

WALK 1

CHINATOWN &
FINANCIAL
DISTRICT

Delancey St-
Essex St

WALK 6

LEGEND

>> SIGHTS & ATTRACTIONS
>> FOOD & DRINK
>> SHOPPING
>> MORE TO EXPLORE

Since it opened in 2009, the **High Line Park**—located on an old train line that runs through the Meatpacking District as well as the Chelsea neighborhood, dozens of feet above street level—has been incredibly popular. Until 1980, the train line was used to bring goods to and from local warehouses. It was slated for demolition in the late 1990s after falling into disuse, until local residents came up with the idea of creating an elevated park. Since most of the buildings in the surrounding area are relatively low, the High Line offers amazing views over the Hudson River and Chelsea.

SHORT ON TIME? HERE ARE THE HIGHLIGHTS
+ TACOMBI + WHITNEY MUSEUM OF AMERICAN ART + CHELSEA MARKET + THE HIGH LINE + NEW MUSEUM

TIPS
// A must-do walk if it's your first time in the Big Apple
// This walk takes you through charming New York City neighborhoods
// Take an evening stroll along the Hudson River

NOLITA, SOHO, WEST VILLAGE & HIGH LINE

1. Love, Adorned
2. Tacombi
3. Thomas Sires
4. Le Labo
5. New Museum
6. Public
7. Erica Weiner
8. The Butcher's Daughter
9. Italian American Museum
10. McNally Jackson Books
11. Saturdays Surf
12. Kate Spade
13. Singer Building
14. 105 Mercer Street
15. Greene Street
16. Film Forum
17. Ellary's Green
18. Prodigy Coffee
19. Stonewall National Monument
20. Greenwich Letterpress
21. Personnel of New York
22. Aesop
23. Wilfie & Nell
24. Mary's Fish Camp
25. Townhouse at 66 Perry Street
26. Aria Wine Bar
27. Magnolia Bakery
28. Whitney Museum of American Art
29. Biergarten
30. Le Bain
31. The High Line
32. Chelsea Market

WALK 2 DESCRIPTION (approx. 4.2 miles)

Begin with shopping on Elizabeth Street ❶ and breakfast at Tacombi, or come back for tacos later in the day ❷. Continue shopping your way down the street ❸ ❹. Turn left on Prince Street toward the New Museum ❺. Head back to Elizabeth Street for Michelin-starred restaurant Public, a jewelry store, and a nice spot for lunch ❻ ❼ ❽. Turn right on Kenmare Street, then make an immediate left on Mott Street. Go right on Grand Street and visit the Italian American Museum ❾. Make a right on Mulberry Street, left on Prince Street for a good selection of books ❿, then left again on Crosby Street ⓫. Turn right on Grand Street, cross Broadway and head right on Mercer Street to check out the fun Kate Spade collection ⓬. Turn right on Spring Street, then make an immediate left on Broadway for some history ⓭. Go left on Prince Street and left again on Mercer Street ⓮. Turn right on Spring Street and check out the cast-iron buildings on Greene Street to the left ⓯. On Thompson Street turn right, and then take a left on West Houston Street to catch a movie ⓰. Turn right on Varick Street, right on Downing Street, and left on Bedford Street. Make a right on Carmine Street for a coffee break or a healthy snack ⓱ ⓲. Go left on Bleecker Street, then right on 7th Avenue South, walking toward Christopher Park ⓳. On the other side of the park you can peruse a lovely card shop ⓴. Continue walking to Greenwich Avenue and then head left ㉑. Make another immediate left on W. 10th Street and walk toward the West Village. Turn left on 7th Avenue South, cross the street at Christopher Park, and continue straight on Christopher Street. Take a right on Bleecker Street ㉒ and then a right on W. 10th Street. To the right is a swell spot for a drink ㉓, or go left on W. 4th Street for good seafood ㉔. Turn left on Perry Street and check out a filming location for TV series Sex and the City ㉕. Continue straight on Perry Street for a bite to eat ㉖. Turn right on Bleecker Street, where you'll find Magnolia Bakery ㉗. Cross to Bethune Street. Turn right on Washington Street and head toward the Meatpacking District. Visit the Whitney on Gansevoort Street ㉘, then relax at Biergarten or at a rooftop bar ㉙ ㉚. Walk over the High Line ㉛ and finish things off with a visit to the Chelsea Market ㉜.

SIGHTS & ATTRACTIONS

⑤ Visit the **New Museum** to see international exhibitions of contemporary art, and to be inspired by creative concepts and innovative ideas. New artists are given a platform for their work here, which often leads to adventurous pieces ranging from sound installations to a simulated spaceship interior. The museum moved to this bigger home on the Bowery in 2007, and you can easily spend hours taking in all the artwork.

235 bowery, www.newmuseum.org, t: (212) 219-1222, open wed & fri-sun 11am-6pm, thu 11am-9pm, entrance $16, j & z trains to bowery, f train to 2nd ave

⑨ This small museum in Little Italy began in 1999 as a temporary exhibit and was met with overwhelming success—leading to the opening of the **Italian American Museum** in 2001. Learn about the historical struggles and successes of Italian Americans through a variety of cultural exhibits.

155 mulberry street, www.italianamericanmuseum.org, t: (212) 965-9000, open fri-sun noon-6pm, mon-thu open to groups by appointment only, minimum donation $5, 6, j, n, q & z trains to canal st

⑬ The **Singer Building** is an excellent place to start if you're looking to explore SoHo's cast-iron architecture. It was erected in 1902 by the Singer Manufacturing Company, known primarily for their sewing machines. Today the building houses numerous offices and apartments.

561 broadway, between prince and spring street, not open to the public, n & r trains to prince st, 6 train to spring st, b, d, f & m trains to broadway-lafayette

⑭ This unassuming house at **105 Mercer Street** has a rather remarkable history. A year after it was built in 1831, it became one of SoHo's thriving brothels. It might be difficult to imagine, but back in the day SoHo was the city's red light district.

105 mercer street, between prince and spring street, not open to the public, n & r trains to prince st, 6 train to spring st, b, d, f & m trains to broadway-lafayette

⑮ You'll find some of SoHo's most beautiful cast-iron buildings on **Greene Street.** The building at #72-76, known as the "King of Greene Street," is one of

the best examples of this type of architecture in the neighborhood. Take a step back to fully admire the tall windows and Corinthian columns.

72-76 greene street, between spring and broome street, c, e & 6 trains to spring st, b, d, f & m trains to broadway-lafayette

㉕ For years the **townhouse at 66 Perry Street** was a backdrop of beloved HBO series *Sex and the City* as protagonist Carrie Bradshaw's apartment building. Although the show was set on the Upper East Side, exterior filming took place here in the West Village and since then, this quaint street has seen a rise in popularity. Every day, countless fans come here to pose for a photo in front of the charming brownstone.

66 perry street, 1 train to christopher st-sheridan sq

㉘ The **Whitney Museum of American Art** holds a collection of America's most diverse forms of artistic expression from the 20th and 21st centuries. See works from Jasper Johns and Andy Warhol, along with everything from paintings and sculptures to videos and performance art. The Whitney Biennial, which spotlights young, undiscovered talents, is particularly well-known. The museum was established in 1931 by wealthy sculptor and art collector Gertrude Vanderbilt Whitney with 700 works from her own collection. Today the permanent collection includes around 18,000 pieces of art. Architect Renzo Piano designed the new Whitney building, which opened in early 2015.

gansevoort street, www.whitney.org, t: (212) 570-3600, open mon, wed & sun 10:30am-6pm, thu-sat 10:30am-10pm, entrance $22, a, c & e trains to 14th st, l train to 8th ave

FOOD & DRINK

② The upbeat atmosphere and delicious food of **Tacombi** make this Mexican taquería a favorite among New Yorkers. Here you'll find authentic tacos, fresh salsa, hearty *huevos*, and fruity drinks right out of an old Volkswagen bus.

267 elizabeth street, www.tacombi.com, t: (917) 727-0179, open sun-wed 11am-midnight, thu-sat 11am-1am, sat-sun breakfast starting at 10am, price $11, b, d, f & m trains to broadway-lafayette

(6) The **Public** building was once a bakery. Upon entering you'll immediately notice the high ceilings, though the space still has an intimate feel. The food here is outstanding, and for several years now the restaurant has held a Michelin star. Public is unfortunately not open for lunch on weekdays, but it's worth coming back this way in the evening for dinner or, if it's the weekend, to indulge in brunch offerings.

210 elizabeth street, www.public-nyc.com, t: (212) 343-7011, open sun-mon 6pm-10pm, thu-sat 6pm-11pm, sat & sun brunch 10:30am-3:30pm, bar open late, price $30, 6 train to spring st, n & r trains to prince st

(8) Head to **The Butcher's Daughter** juice bar and café for a yummy breakfast, healthy lunch, fresh juice, or smoothie. Despite what the name suggests, don't expect to find any giant slabs of meat here; according to the restaurant, it treats fruits and vegetables "as a butcher would meat." The interior has a rugged, industrial look but with a fresh, feminine twist. In the summertime, the restaurant sets up long picnic tables outside.

19 kenmare street, www.thebutchersdaughter.com, t: (212) 219-3434, open mon-thu & sun 8am-10pm, fri-sat 8am-11pm, price $11, j & z trains to bowery

(17) The owner of **Ellary's Greens** is a hospitable woman who only serves food in her restaurant that she'd serve her own family. The menu accommodates a variety of diets, including vegetarian, vegan, and gluten-free. A spot by the window—which is always open in the summer—is a popular place to perch.

33 carmine street, www.ellarysgreens.com, t: (212) 920-5072, open mon-fri 9am-11pm, sat 10am-11pm, sun 10am-10pm, price $15, a, b, c, d, f & m trains to w 4th st, 1 train to christopher st

(18) Good, fair-trade coffee is the philosophy at **Prodigy Coffee.** This small café (it has just a few tables) offers a selection of yummy pastries, too.

33 carmine street, www.prodigycoffee.com, t: (212) 414-4142, open mon-fri 7am-7pm, sat-sun 8am-7pm, price coffee from $2.50, a, b, c, d, e & f trains to w 4th st

(23) Casual West Village bar **Wilfie & Nell** is a happening spot in the evenings after work and on the weekends until late. People come here for a drink and a chat with those around them, whether tourists or locals. It's often standing-room

only here, although there are some stools at the bar.

228 west 4th street, www.wilfieandnell.com, t: (212) 242-2990, open mon-wed 4pm-3am, thu-fri 4pm-4am, sat-sun noon-4am, price $9, 1 & 2 trains to christopher st, a, b, c, d, e, f & m trains to w 4th st

(24) As soon as you walk in the door at **Mary's Fish Camp,** you'll feel as if you're on the water thanks to the crisp blue interior and smell of fresh fish. It has an extensive menu and, on Mondays, you can get a nice bottle of wine with your meal for just $20—a great price by NYC standards.

64 charles street, www.marysfishcamp.com, t: (646) 486-2185, open mon-sat noon-3pm & 6pm-11pm, sun noon-4pm, price $22, 1 & 2 trains to christopher st, a, b, c, d, e, f & m trains to w 4th st

(26) **Aria Wine Bar** serves up high-quality Italian food. The open bar makes for a laidback atmosphere, as do the rustic wooden tables, white tiles, and untreated brick walls. It's always hopping here, so be sure to arrive early.

117 perry street, fb: nycaria, t: (212) 242-4233, open daily 11am-midnight, price pasta $12, 1 train to christopher st, 1, 2 & 3 trains to 14th st

(29) You'll find **Biergarten** tucked away under the High Line in The Standard hotel. It draws a mix of neighborhood locals, tourists, and New York City professionals. Come here to relax with a drink or play an old-fashioned game of ping-pong. Be sure to bring along your ID.

848 washington street, www.standardhotels.com, t: (212) 645-4646, open mon-wed & sun noon-1am, thu-sat noon-2am, price $8, a, c & e trains to 14th st, l train to 8th ave

(30) **Le Bain,** also in The Standard, is a trendy rooftop bar. It's fairly easy to get in during the week; on weekends, you'll have to don your finest threads and try your luck. Who knows, maybe you'll bump into someone famous.

848 washington street, in the standard hotel, www.standardhotels.com, t: (212) 645-4646, open mon 4pm-midnight, tue-thu 4pm-4am, fri-sat 2pm-4am, sun 2pm-3am, price drinks from $12, a, c & e trains to 14th st, l train to 8th ave

㉜ Oreo cookies were once made on the site of today's **Chelsea Market.** Now people go to this old factory space for good food and shopping. There are lots of options, but we recommend the lobster roll at Lobster Place. Look for a place to sit in the hall and people watch while you eat. If there are no free tables, take your food outside and head up to the High Line.

75 ninth avenue, www.chelseamarket.com, t: (888) 727-7887, open mon-sat 7am-9pm, sun 8am-8pm, a, c & e trains to 14th st

SHOPPING

① The neon lights on the shelves are reason alone to stop and take a look inside **Love, Adorned.** This gorgeous store is a great place to come for unique jewelry, home decor, travel accessories, personal care products, and art.

269 elizabeth street, www.loveadorned.com, t: (212) 431-5683, open daily noon-8pm, b, d, f & m trains to broadway-lafayette

③ The **Thomas Sires** collection is an eclectic combination of items. In this spacious boutique with whitewashed walls you'll find Japanese bed linens, stylish clothes for women and children, and beautiful toys. The items from Peru are especially unique and popular.

243 elizabeth street, www.thomassires.com, t: (646) 692-4472, open mon-sat noon-7pm, sun noon-6pm, b, d, f & m trains to broadway-lafayette

④ NY-based **Le Labo** is a fragrance laboratory, complete with old workbenches, bottle-lined shelves, and vintage cases. Let the lab create a unique fragrance for you on the spot from a mix of natural ingredients, and add your own initials to the bottle for an extra personal touch. It also has a City Exclusives line featuring perfumes generally only sold in stores in the cities after which they're named, including one made just for New York.

233 elizabeth street, www.lelabofragrances.com, t: (212) 219-2230, open daily 11am-7pm, f train to 2nd ave, j train to bowery

⑦ Jewelry maker **Erica Weiner** was able to turn her hobby into a career, and in 2006 she traded in her workspace at a kitchen table for her very own store. She

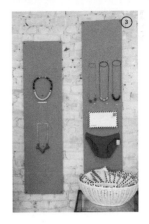

Antique pen nibs
on brass chain.
Steel 45.
Gold 60.

sells all types of jewelry, including antique, vintage, and new items. Necklaces and rings are beautifully displayed in this charming shop.

173 elizabeth street, www.ericaweiner.com, t: (212) 334-6383, open daily noon-7pm, 6 train to spring st, j train to bowery

⑩ With just two floors, **McNally Jackson Books** is a far cry from the largest bookstore in New York. It does have one of the best selections, however, and the store aspires to be "the center of Manhattan's literary culture." Grab a seat on a comfortable sofa and thumb through a book or magazine. The store also has a café that sells good coffee, sandwiches, and quiches.

52 prince street, www.mcnallyjackson.com, t: (212) 274-1160, open mon-sat 10am-10pm, sun 10am-9pm, b, d, f & m trains to broadway-lafayette, n & r trains to prince st

⑪ You might not expect to come across a surf shop in New York City, but that is exactly what you'll find at **Saturdays Surf.** This funky shop is a unique combination of surf supplies, art, books, clothing, and accessories, with a good espresso bar. Enjoy your coffee and a moment of calm on the terrace out back.

31 crosby street, www.saturdaysnyc.com, t: (212) 966-7875, open mon-sun 10am-7pm, j, n, q, z & 6 trains to canal st, 6 train to spring st

⑫ You can't help but feel happy when you see the colorful **Kate Spade** collection. In this store you'll find everything you need for a weekend away, from quirky clothes and bags to travel accessories with a twist.

454 broome street, www.katespade.com, t: (212) 274-1991, open mon-sat 10am-8pm, sun 11am-7pm, 6 train to spring st

⑳ Whatever occasion you're shopping for, **Greenwich Letterpress** is bound to have something for you. Nearly all of the cards are designed and printed in-house using a letterpress, the classic relief printing technique that's experiencing a revival.

39 christopher street, www.greenwichletterpress.com, t: (212) 989-7464, open mon 1pm-6pm, tue-fri 11am-7pm, sat-sun noon-6pm, 1 train to christopher st

㉑ At **Personnel of New York** you'll find designer clothes, jewelry, and lifestyle products for men and women. The store is run by a couple who selects the store's collection from local designers they know. Be sure to also check out the unique Art Deco storefront.

9 greenwich avenue, www.personnelofnewyork.com, t: (212) 924-0604, open mon-sat 11am-8pm, sun noon-7pm, 1 & 2 trains to cristopher st, a, b, c, d, e, f & m trains to w 4th st

㉒ Australia-based **Aesop**'s skin and hair care products not only smell amazing but are nicely packaged, too. Each store has a unique interior adapted to suit the neighborhood where it's located; but the underlying design style is always recognizable: Pure and stylish with earthy colors.

341 bleecker street, www.aesop.com, t: (212) 899-3359, open mon-wed & sun 11am-7pm, thu-sat 11am-8pm, 1, 2, 3, a, b, d, e, f & m trains to christopher st

㉗ You'll know you're close to **Magnolia Bakery** when you see people walking by carrying white boxes. Inside are the delicious cupcakes made famous by *Sex and the City*. If you're not in the mood for a cupcake, try the banana pudding.

401 bleecker street, www.magnoliabakery.com, t: (212) 462-2572, open mon-thu 9am-11:30pm, fri-sat 9am-12:30am, sun 9am-11:30pm, price cupcake $3.25, a, c, e & l trains to 14th street, 1 train to christopher st

MORE TO EXPLORE

⑯ From Fellini to Fassbinder, **Film Forum** shows it all. This is one of the best places in New York City for foreign films and documentaries.

209 west houston street, near varick street, www.filmforum.org, t: (212) 727-8110, open daily 12:30pm-11:30pm, price ticket $13, 1 train to houston st

⑲ In June of 1969, a violent clash at the Stonewall Inn sparked the modern fight for gay and lesbian equality in the United States. The bar and the surrounding area, near Christopher Park, were designated as the **Stonewall National Monument** by former President Obama in 2016. The park is a nice place to relax, and the surrounding vicinity, especially Christopher Street, harbors a variety of gay bars and shops.

7th avenue and christopher street, 1 train to christopher st/sheridan sq

㉛ A trip to the **High Line,** an elevated park built on a former train viaduct, feels like walking over a giant balcony that extends through the city. The park is dozens of feet above street level and stretches from Gansevoort Street to W. 34th Street. From up here you can look out over the Hudson River, old warehouses, and the streets of Manhattan.

from gansevoort street to 34th street, between 10th and 11th avenue, www.thehighline.org, t: (212) 500-6035, open daily dec-march 7am-7pm, april-may & oct-nov 7am-10pm, june-sept 7am-11pm, free entrance, a, c, e & l trains to 8th ave/14th st

WALK 3

TIMES SQUARE & UNION SQUARE

ABOUT THE WALK

This walk emphasizes art and culture, routing you past MoMA, the Museum of Arts and Design, and the unique architecture of Grand Central Terminal. For those who love shopping, there's also upscale Fifth Avenue. Be aware that it gets incredibly busy around Times Square, with its theaters and popular retail stores. It's somewhat calmer here on weekdays, except at lunchtime.

THE NEIGHBORHOODS

New York is known the world over for **Times Square,** where yellow cabs cruise past giant screens and neon lights. For more than 100 years people have flocked to this area for entertainment, including everything from opera and vaudeville to comedy and musicals. In the 1960s and 1970s, gambling dens and sex shows were on nearly every corner. The area was later redeveloped—which some refer to as the Disneyfication of Times Square—and began drawing in a far different crowd from its former days, creating a more inviting atmosphere for tourists attending theaters, entertainment venues, and retail stores.

Broadway cuts right through Times Square. Here you can catch renowned shows like *The Lion King, Wicked, The Book of Mormon,* and *Hamilton* (if you can manage to finagle tickets to the perenially sold-out show!). Discounted tickets are available for many shows at the TKTS Booth, where lines form daily.

Other icons of this mostly Midtown Manhattan walk include Rockefeller Center, Grand Central Terminal, the Museum of Modern Art (MoMA), Radio City Music Hall, **Fifth Avenue,** and the **Empire State Building.**

Further south lies **Gramercy Park,** a neighborhood named for its pretty, private park, which is accessible exclusively to key-holding local residents; however, the quaint and leafy surrounding area makes for a pleasant stroll.

At Union Square, uptown/downtown and east side/west side converge. Play a game of chess with a stranger, admire the work of local artists, or grab food and a drink at the great restaurants and bars in the area. It's also an excellent spot to simply sit and people watch. Union Square is also known for its Greenmarket, a lively farmers market.

SHORT ON TIME? HERE ARE THE HIGHLIGHTS
**+ MOMA + ROCKEFELLER CENTER + NEW YORK PUBLIC LIBRARY
+ BRYANT PARK + GRAND CENTRAL TERMINAL**

TIPS
// A must-do walk if it's your first time in the Big Apple // Allow yourself plenty of time for the many stellar museums on this route // Visit the Empire State Building extra early or very late at night

WALK 3 DESCRIPTION (approx. 7.8 miles)

Begin the walk at the Museum of Arts and Design ❶. Then walk to the right, keeping Central Park on your left. Turn right on 7th Avenue, then left on 56th Street for a tasty burger ❷. Go left on 6th Avenue, then right on Central Park South. At the corner of the famous Fifth Avenue you'll see a historic hotel ❸. Cross Fifth Avenue, where the streets are lined with shops and security for Trump Tower ❹. Go right on Lexington Avenue and grab a sandwich and delicious espresso ❺. Turn right on 53rd Street to find a piece of the Berlin Wall and visit the MoMA ❻ ❼. Walk between the buildings across from MoMA and emerge at 52nd Street. Turn left here to learn about TV and radio ❽. Continue walking to Fifth Avenue and then go right to visit a church ❾. Between 50th and 49th Street, turn right and walk down the shopping promenade. You'll see Rockefeller Center towering in front of you ❿ ⓫. Continue on 50th Street ⓬. On 6th Avenue turn left, then right on 47th Street toward the bustling center of NYC ⓭. Turn left on 7th Avenue and left again on 43rd Street. Photography fans will want to make a detour on 6th Avenue ⓮, then go back down the street and turn left on 42nd Street to visit a park and see some historic buildings ⓯ ⓰ ⓱. Head up the stairs on the west side of Grand Central Terminal for a cocktail ⓲. Exit the station on Lexington Avenue and be sure to look up ⓳. Head back to Park Avenue, turn left, and continue to 36th Street. Turn right here to visit a museum ⓴. Take another left on Fifth Avenue, where an amazing view of the city awaits ㉑. Continue on Fifth Avenue. Turn left on 30th Street and you'll find Dover Street Market ㉒. Head back to Fifth Avenue, then take a left and an immediate right on 29th Street for coffee or a bite to eat ㉓ ㉔. Turn left and left again to get back to Fifth Avenue for cocktails at a rooftop bar ㉕. Continue on through Madison Square Park ㉖ ㉗. Head down Broadway and take a left on 20th Street to take in some history ㉘. Then go back to Broadway for some shopping ㉙ ㉚. Take a left on 19th Street. Turn left on Park Avenue, then right on 20th Street ㉛. Make a right on Irving Place and continue to 16th Street. Turn right for Union Square ㉜ ㉝ and end with dinner on 13th Street ㉞.

SIGHTS & ATTRACTIONS

① The **Museum of Arts and Design (MAD)** is a large museum with some 2,000 items in its permanent collection alone, including fashion, design, and jewelry objects. MAD is also known for its radical building renovation, which was not well received in the architecture world. Much criticism focused on the windows, which appear to spell out a banal messsage: "Hi." On the flip side, it does offer diners in the ninth-floor restaurant excellent views of Central Park.

2 columbus circle, www.madmuseum.org, t: (212) 299-7777, open tue-wed & sat-sun 10am-6pm, thu-fri 10am-9pm, entrance $16, 1, a, b, c & d trains to columbus circle

③ Many a famous person has stayed at the **Plaza Hotel.** Architect Frank Lloyd Wright, for example, stayed here while designing the Guggenheim. Rooms on the north side of the hotel have great views of Central Park. If you're spruced up enough you could probably steal a peek of the lobby. Around the corner you'll find the entrance to the Plaza Food Hall, a genuine feast for the eyes and mouth.

768 5th avenue, www.theplaza.com, t: (212) 759-3000, lobby open to public, n, q & r trains to lexington ave/59th st, 4, 5 & 6 trains to 59th st

④ Spanning over 6 miles, **Fifth Avenue** is one of New York's most iconic streets. A walk from the beginning at Washington Square Arch in Washington Square Park to the end at 143rd Street and Harlem River Drive, in upper Harlem, takes approximately 2.5 hours, leading past major attractions including the Flat- iron Building, Empire State Building, New York Public Library, Rockefeller Centre, Central Park, and Museum Mile. But for most visitors, shopping is still the main attraction. Between 34th and 60th Street you'll find countless high-end stores, including Lord & Taylor and Bergdorf Goodman, and flagships for brands such as Tiffany & Co., Apple, Lego, and Gucci. Trump Tower also sits on this famous stretch, so expect a security detail around the president's New York home base, including barriers and bag checks.

5th avenue, www.visit5thavenue.com, n & r trains to 5th ave/59th st

⑥ A small piece of the **Berlin Wall** now stands in Midtown Manhattan. Feel free to take a seat at one of the tables and rest a while.

west 53rd street, between madison and 5th avenue, e & m trains to 5th ave/53rd st

⑦ The world-famous **Museum of Modern Art (MoMA)** has an extensive and unique collection of contemporary and modern art. There is plenty to see here, such as a helicopter suspended from the ceiling, a collection of old computers, works by Picasso, and video art. Don't forget to also visit the **MoMA Design Store.**

11 west 53rd street, between 5th and 6th avenue, www.moma.org, t: (212) 708-9400, open sat-mon & tue-thu 10:30am-5:30pm, fri 10:30am-8pm, entrance $25, e & m trains to 5th ave/53rd st, b, d & e trains to 7th ave

⑧ Learn all about the history of radio and television at the **Paley Center for Media.** Watch and listen to a Sinatra concert, re-experience the first *Star Trek* episode, or enjoy a documentary.

25 west 52nd street, between 5th and 6th avenue, www.paleycenter.org, t: (212) 621-6800, open wed noon-6pm, thu noon-8pm, fri-sun noon-6pm, entrance $10, e & m trains to 5th ave/53rd st, b, d, f & m trains to 47th-50th st/rockefeller ctr

⑨ The impressive **St. Patrick's Cathedral,** built in 1879, is the largest Gothic cathedral in the United States—it can fit more than 2,000 people inside. Be sure to check out the Tiffany altars, stained-glass windows, and pietà, the statue of Mary holding Jesus's body.

14 east 51st street, at 5th avenue, www.saintpatrickscathedral.org, t: (212) 753-2261, open daily 6:30am-8:45pm, free entrance, e & m trains to 5th ave/53rd st, b, d, f & m trains to 47th-50th st/rockefeller ctr

⑩ The world-famous **NBC Studios** have been home to radio broadcasts since 1933, and television since its invention. The location was immortalized on the popular sitcom *30 Rock,* and today is best known for airing *The Tonight Show starring Jimmy Fallon* and *Saturday Night Live.* Dedicated fans can enter the ticket lottery months in advance, or queue for stand-by tickets at 7am on the morning of the show. Throngs of people can often be seen trying to catch a glimpse of the celebrities appearing in the live broadcasts. You can take a tour behind the scenes and visit The Shop at NBC Studios to pick up souvenirs.

30 rockefeller plaza, www.thetouratnbcstudios.com, t: (212) 664-3700 tours/ (212) 664-3056 tickets, tours mon-fri 8:20am-2pm, sat-sun 8:20am-5pm, price tour $33, e & m trains to 5th ave/53rd st, b, d, f & m trains to 47th-50th st/rockefeller ctr

⑪ John D. Rockefeller bought a piece of property in 1928 that he developed to include office buildings and public promenades. He named it **Rockefeller Center.** Come here in the winter to go ice skating next to the giant Christmas tree. Don't pass up a trip to the Top of the Rock observation deck, where you'll have an unobstructed view of Central Park and the Empire State Building.

5th to 7th avenue, from 47th to 51st street, www.rockefellercenter.com, t: (212) 692-7625, open daily 7am-midnight, entrance $30 for top of the rock, e & m trains to 5th ave/53rd st, b, d, f & m trains to 47th-50th st/rockefeller ctr

⑬ With its bright lights, enormous billboards, and constant crowds, **Times Square** is the pulse of New York City. Under the red stairs you'll find the **TKTS Booth,** where you can buy discounted tickets for shows on and off Broadway; sometimes you can get up to 50% off. Go early, as lines can be long.

broadway and 7th avenue, between 42nd and 47th street, www.tdf.org, t: (212) 768-1560, open mon & fri 3pm-8pm, tue 2pm-8pm, wed-thu & sat 10am-8pm, sun 11am-7pm, n, q, r, s, 1, 2, 3 & 7 trains to times sq/42nd st

⑭ Take a trip to the **International Center of Photography** and see unique photos from around the world. There are always plenty of notable temporary exhibits here.

1133 6th avenue, at 43rd street, www.icp.org, t: (718) 486-7372, open mon-fri 9am-7pm, sat 9am-3pm, sun 9:30am-1:30pm, entrance $14, b, d, f & m trains to 42nd st/bryant pk

⑯ The largest branch of the **New York Public Library** opened in 1911 and is located in the Stephen A. Schwarzman Building. In the 1930s, Mayor Fiorello LaGuardia gave the marble lions that sit outside the building the nicknames Patience and Fortitude, emphasizing the qualities New Yorkers needed to endure during the Depression.

5th avenue, at 42nd street, www.nypl.org, t: (917) 275-6975, open mon, fri-sat 10am-6pm, tue-wed, thu 10am-8pm, free entrance, n, q, r, s, 1, 2 & 3 trains to times sq/42nd st, b, d, f & m trains to 42nd st, 7 train to 5th ave

⑰ **Grand Central Terminal** is a Beaux Art masterpiece embodying the romanticism of train travel. The annual Holiday Laser Light Show projected on the

ceiling of the main hall, which begins on November 30 and runs for six weeks, is particularly impressive.

87 east 42nd street, between madison and lexington avenue, www.grandcentral terminal.com, t: (212) 953-0409, open daily 5:30am-2am, s, 4, 5, 6 & 7 trains to grand central/42nd st

(19) The **Chrysler Building** is the crowning achievement of auto industry giant Walter P. Chrysler. Designs of hubcaps and fenders have been incorporated into the building both inside and out. You'll also find water spouts shaped like radiator caps. The 1,046-foot-tall building is a unique Art Deco monument. It was the tallest building in the world when it opened in 1000. One year later, it was dethroned by the Empire State Building.

405 lexington avenue, between 42nd and 43rd street, not open to the public, s, 4, 5, 6 & 7 trains to grand central/42nd st

(20) The wonderful collection at **The Morgan Library & Museum** comes from wealthy banker and art collector John Pierpont Morgan's private collection. In 1924, 11 years after his death, it was opened up to the public. The collection includes manuscripts, drawings, books, and old Middle Eastern tablets.

225 madison avenue, at 36th street, www.themorgan.org, t: (212) 685-0008, open tue-thu 10:30am-5pm, fri 10:30am-9pm, sat 10am-6pm, sun 11am-6pm, entrance $18, 6 train to 33rd st, s, 4, 5, 6 & 7 trains to grand central

(21) The **Empire State Building** is the result of a competition between the chairmen of General Motors and Chrysler to see who could be the first to build the world's tallest building. The pencil-shaped building opened in 1931 and, until 1971, was indeed the tallest building in the world. The Empire State Building is the third-tallest building in New York and the fifth-tallest in the United States. The view from the 86th floor is phenomenal.

350 5th avenue, between 33rd and 34th street, www.esbnyc.com, open daily 8am-2am (last elevators up at 1:15am), entrance $32, 1, 2 & 3 trains to 34th st/penn station, b, d, f, n, q & r trains to 34th st/herald sq

(27) The **Flatiron Building** was designed in 1902 in an attempt to establish a new business district north of Wall Street, and sits perfectly on a triangular, iron-

shaped plot of land. The 22-story landmark building is considered to be a ground-breaking skyscraper: Upon completion it was one of the tallest constructions in the city. There's often a strong, unpredictable wind around the building; back in the day, young boys would wait around here in the hopes of catching a glimpse of a summer skirt swept up by the gales.

175 5th avenue, at 23rd street, not open to the public, n & r trains to 23rd st

㉘ Former president Theodore Roosevelt lived on 20th Street as a young boy. The **Theodore Roosevelt Birthplace,** a reconstruction of the house, is an interesting place to visit for history buffs and Roosevelt fans alike.

28 east 20th street, between broadway and park avenue south, www.nyharbor parks.org/visit/thro.html, t: (212) 854-1754, open tue-sat 10am-5pm, tours each hour on the hour, free entrance, 6, n & r trains to 23rd st

㉛ **Gramercy Park** is the only non-public park in New York; the keys are exclusively available to parkside residents. In the 19th century, most apartments were intended for the poor. The apartments at **34 Gramercy Park East** were therefore called "French flats" to distinguish them from those where the working class lived. Go for a drink on the beautiful terrace of the Gramercy Park Hotel.

20th street, east of park avenue, not open to the public, 6 train to 23rd st

FOOD & DRINK

② Walk into the lobby of Le Parker Meridien Hotel and you'll think it's a bit boring. But peek behind the red curtain and you'll discover the fabulous, retro **Burger Joint.** The menu here is simple: hamburger or cheeseburger. It's uncomplicated but oh, so delicious.

119 west 56th street, www.parkermeridien.com/eat4.php, t: (212) 708-7414, open sun 11am-11:30pm, fri-sat 11am-midnight, price burgers from $9 (cash only), n, q & r trains to 57th st/7th ave, f train to 57th st

⑤ From out on bustling Lexington Avenue, the smell of fresh coffee will lure you into **Little Collins.** This charming espresso bar is the perfect place to unwind. It makes the most delicious espresso in town, with milk straight from the

farm. Hankering for a bite to eat? Try the Smash—tasty avocado and feta on toast.

667 lexington avenue, www.littlecollinsnyc.com, t: (212) 308-1969, open mon-fri 7am-5pm, sat-sun 8am-4pm, price $10, e & m trains to lexington ave/53rd st

⑱ **Campbell Apartment** is a stylish, old-school bar tucked away in the heart of Grand Central Terminal. The people who come here after work during the week are always dressed to a T. The clientele is more diverse on the weekend, but sneakers are never allowed.

grand central terminal, near southwest balcony, www.hospitalityholdings.com, t: (212) 953-0409, open mon-thu noon-1am, fri-sat noon-2am, sun noon-midnight, price drinks $14, s, 4, 5, 6 & 7 trains to grand central/42nd st

㉓ The first branch of **Stumptown Coffee Roasters** in New York is located in the trendy Ace Hotel. This rock and roll coffee house may only have a few locations in the U.S., but it's well-known among creative types and coffee snobs alike. Order yours and drink it right in the hotel lobby. The beans are top quality, so don't expect any frappuccino-like concoctions here. Cool baristas will brew your cup using old-school techniques and precision.

18 west 29th street, www.stumptowncoffee.com, t: (718) 782-0910, open mon-fri 6am-8pm, sat-sun 7am-8pm, price coffee from $3.40 (cash only), n & r trains to 28th st

(24) The **John Dory Oyster Bar** is the place to go for oysters. Here you'll also find the best lobster sandwich in the city: the JDOB lobster roll. The restaurant also has a nice selection of various types of raw fish, and the small dishes are great to share. The playful and imaginative interior was designed by the same person responsible for the Ace Hotel and The Dutch.

1196 broadway, at 29th street, www.thejohndory.com, t: (212) 792-9000, kitchen open mon-sun noon-midnight, bar open late, price $21, n & r trains to 28th st

(25) From the roof of **230 Fifth** you can gaze through the palm trees out onto the Empire State Building and lower Manhattan. The atmosphere and view here make for a truly remarkable experience. In the winter, enjoy the same amazing view from inside the bar one floor down.

230 5th avenue, at 27th street, www.230-fifth.com, t: (212) 725-4300, open mon-fri 4pm-4am, sat-sun 10am-4am (21 and up only), price $16, cocktails from $14, 6 train to 33rd st, b, d, f & m trains to 34th st/herald sq

(26) Enjoy a delicious hamburger at **Shake Shack.** Multiple Shake Shacks are now spread across the city, but it all began right here in Madison Square Park. New Yorkers are prepared to wait over an hour for these hamburgers, but thanks to the Shack Cam—which shows real-time views of the line—you may not have to. If the line's long, do a loop through the park.

madison square park, corner of madison avenue and east 23rd street, www.shake shack.com, t: (212) 889-6600, open daily 11am-11pm, price $13, n, r & 6 trains to 23rd st

(32) Contrary to what the name suggests, you can get much more than just coffee at **The Coffee Shop.** Open nearly round the clock on certain days, this café has an extensive dinner menu and serves up traditional American fare at a reasonable price. Come here for late-night scrambled eggs and rub elbows with the city's

other hip night owls. One of the highlights during the day is the terrace outside. The Coffee Shop is also a popular spot for a drink and burger after work.

29 union square west, www.thecoffeeshopnyc.com, t: (212) 243-7969, open mon-fri midnight-11pm, sat-sun 24 hours, price $17, l, n, q, r, 5 & 6 trains to union sq

(34) It's easy to spend an entire evening around the table at upscale Venetian restaurant **All'onda.** It's somewhat hidden behind Union Square, so the crowd here is primarily just locals. The restaurant has two floors and a bar downstairs. The tuna and *agnolotti* are highly recommended.

22 east 13th street, www.allondanyc.com, t: (212) 231-2236, dinner tue-sun 5:30pm-11pm, brunch sat-sun 11:30am-2:30pm, price $30, n, r, o, l, 4, 5 & 6 trains to 15th st/union sq, n, r, o, l, 4, 5 & 6 trains to 15th st/union sq

SHOPPING

(22) You'll find the entrance to the **Dover Street Market** down a small street between Park and Lexington Avenue. It's easy to endlessly shop in this six-floor store designed by Rei Kawakubo of Comme des Garçons. Items from top fashion labels are beautifully displayed here. Take the elevator all the way to the top, then work your way down floor by floor.

160 lexington avenue, www.newyork.doverstreetmarket.com, t: (646) 837-7750, open mon-sat 11am-7pm, sun noon-6pm, 6 train to 28th st

(29) At first glance, **Fishs Eddy** may seem to sell just your average dinnerware, but nothing could be further from the truth. Check out the humorous window displays and be sure to control yourself inside—there are some clever designs in this shop. Products include everything from patterned glassware to kitchen towels with iconic NYC buildings on them, making this a great place to pick up unique souvenirs.

889 broadway, www.fishseddy.com, t: (212) 420-9020, open mon-thu 9am-9pm, fri-sat 9am-10am, sun 10am-8pm, n & r trains to 23rd st

(30) Those with an interest in interior design, or just design in general, will not want to miss **ABC Carpet & Home.** The window displays all have unique

themes, and the style inside is inspiring. The store sells home decor, lifestyle products, jewelry, and furniture. Each floor of the store is styled differently, but always with the latest trends in mind. Downstairs you'll find **ABC Kitchen,** a serene space with amazing food.

888 & 881 broadway, www.abchome.com, t: (212) 473-3000, open mon-wed & fri-sat 10am-7pm, thu 10am-8pm, sun 11am-6:30pm, n & r trains to 23rd st

MORE TO EXPLORE

⑫ **Radio City Music Hall** is the largest covered theater in the world and a beautiful example of Art Deco. One of the most popular events is The Christmas Spectacular, with legendary precision dance company The Rockettes.

1260 6th avenue, between 50th and 51st street, www.radiocity.com, t: (212) 307-7171, tickets on sale mon-sun 11:30am-6pm, see website for program and prices, b, d, f & m trains to 47th-50th st/rockefeller ctr

⑮ Head to **Bryant Park** for some rest and relaxation. Grab a coffee and a snack at one of the kiosks and then sit back and take in the skyscrapers around you. At the east end of the park is the Bryant Park Café, one of the city's most popular outdoor bars. There are open-air movies every Monday night in the summer.
42nd street and 6th avenue, www.bryantpark.org, open daily from 7am, n, q, r, s, 1, 2 & 3 trains to times sq/42nd st, b, d, f & m trains to 42nd st/7th/5th ave, s, 4, 5, 6 to grand central/42nd st

㉝ The **Union Square Greenmarket** began in 1976 with a handful of farmers and has since grown into an enormous market where, during peak season, some 140 regional farmers come to sell their products. Vendors sell organic fruits and vegetables, bread, cheese, and organic wine. Check out the cooking demonstrations from famous local chefs and sample their creations.
union square, www.grownyc.org/greenmarket/manhattan-union-square, open mon, wed, fri, sat 8am-6pm, n, r, q, l, 5 & 6 trains to union sq

WALK 4

UPPER EAST SIDE & CENTRAL PARK

ABOUT THE WALK

This is an ideal walk for those with a penchant for art and nature. The route covers what is known as Museum Mile and takes you past all of the big museums on the east side of the city, including the Guggenheim and the Met. You'll discover amazing art collections and exhibitions. The route will also take you through beautiful Central Park, where you can escape the hustle and bustle of the city. Head to the park for a nice picnic or bike ride.

THE NEIGHBORHOODS

The stretch of Fifth Avenue east of lower Central Park is known as Manhattan's **"Gold Coast."** The area has an incredibly high concentration of private clubs, exclusive schools, art institutions, and millionaires with far-reaching influence. No other neighborhood in the country donates as much to national political campaigns as the Upper East Side.

The beautiful townhouses lining the avenues and streets near Central Park were once the residences of wealthy businesspeople who made their fortunes in steel, oil, and finance. Many of these houses are today home to cultural institutions, embassies, schools, and museums—although a fair amount are still the homes of well-heeled New Yorkers. East of Park Avenue the neighborhood is more down to earth and much livelier. On Lexington Avenue you'll find lots of bustling stores and restaurants frequented by young couples and families from the neighborhood.

Those who enjoy museums are in the right place on the Upper East Side. The neighborhood is home to such renowned museums as **The Metropolitan Museum of Art,** the **Guggenheim,** the **Neue Galerie,** and the **Frick Collection,** which contain some of the most beautiful art collections in the world. These museums line Fifth Avenue, garnering the nickname Museum Mile.

On Madison Avenue you'll find countless galleries, jewelers, and exclusive stores and boutiques from top designers. Department stores Barneys and Bloomingdale's are also located here, and shoppers can regularly be spotted walking down the street with their Little and Big Brown Bags.

SHORT ON TIME? HERE ARE THE HIGHLIGHTS
+ GUGGENHEIM MUSEUM + NEUE GALERIE + THE METROPOLITAN MUSEUM OF ART + THE LOEB BOATHOUSE + BETHESDA TERRACE

TIPS
// This walk offers a good mix of art & nature
// Perfect for a Sunday
// The walk can be broken up into parts

UPPER EAST SIDE & CENTRAL PARK

1. Bloomingdale's
2. Sprinkles Cupcake ATM
3. The Bar Room
4. Barneys
5. The Metropolitan Club
6. The Pierre
7. Knickerbocker Club
8. Edith & Ernesto Fabbri House
9. 726 Madison Avenue
10. Central Park Zoo
11. Wollman Rink
12. Heckscher Ballfields
13. Roosevelt House
14. The East Pole
15. 7th Regiment Armory
16. The west side of Park Avenue, from 68th to 69th Street
17. Frick Collection
18. Christian Louboutin
19. Café Carlyle
20. Butterfield Express
21. La Maison du Chocolat
22. The Jewish Museum
23. Cooper Hewitt, Smithsonian Design Museum
24. Guggenheim Museum
25. Neue Galerie
26. 1040 5th Avenue
27. Metropolitan Museum of Art
28. E.A.T.
29. Central Park Bicycle Rental
30. The Loeb Boathouse
31. Bethesda Fountain/Bethesda Terrace
32. Naumburg Bandshell/The Mall

UPPER
WEST SIDE

86th St

86th St

79th St

Hayden
Planetarium

American Mus.
Natural History

81st St-
Museum of
Natural History

WALK 5

72nd St

Belvedere Castle

Turtle
Pond

The Lake

72nd St

Central

Park

Jacqueline Kennedy
Onassis Reservoir

RESERVOIR RUNNING TK

RESERVOIR RUNNING TRACK

Jewish Museum

Cooper-Hewitt,
Smithsonian Design Mus.

Guggenheim
Museum

Neue Galerie
New York

The Metropolitan
Museum of Art

96th St

86th St

WALK 4

UPPER
EAST SIDE

American Folk
Art Mus.

56th St-
Center

American Folk
Art Mus.

Mus. of Arts
and Design

St-Columbus Circle

57th St-7th Av

7th Av

Sheep
Meadow

The Mall

Tisch's Children Zoo
Crime Busters Rock

The Pond

FINISH

Whitney Mus. of
American Art

Frick Collection

68th St-Hunter
College

Lexington Av-
63rd Street

MIDTOWN
(CENTRAL PARK,
TIMES SQUARE &
UNION SQUARE)

American Folk
Art Mus.

Mus. of
Modern Art

Radio City

WALK 3

59th St-
5th Av

59th St

59th St-
Lexington Av

START

77th St

John Jay
Park

0   250

WALK 4 DESCRIPTION (approx. 6.4 miles)

Start on Lexington Avenue with some shopping at Bloomingdale's ❶, then get a cupcake out of the cupcake ATM ❷. Turn right on 60th Street, past a bar-restaurant to keep in mind for the evening ❸. Continue walking and turn right on Madison Avenue for some shopping ❹. Then head back to 60th Street ❺ and turn right at Central Park past The Pierre and Knickerbocker Club ❻ ❼. Turn right on 62nd Street to #11 ❽. Then go left on Madison Avenue and check out #726 ❾. Head left on 64th Street and into Central Park, the city's backyard. When the weather is nice, people flock here in droves to bike, jog, walk, do yoga, and visit the Central Park Zoo, Wollman Rink, and Heckscher Ballfields ❿ ⓫ ⓬. Exit the park at 65th Street ⓭ and continue straight for a nice lunch ⓮. Turn left on Lexington Avenue, left again, and then right to the 7th Regiment Armory ⓯ and the west side of Park Avenue ⓰. Turn left on 70th Street. At the end of the street you'll find the Frick Collection ⓱. Go right on 5th Avenue along Central Park, then right on 73rd Street and left on Madison Avenue for some shoe shopping ⓲. Turn right on 76th Street if you're looking for an Upper East Side-style meal ⓳. Head left on Lexington Avenue and pick up some delicious food if you'd prefer a picnic ⓴. Then turn left on 78th Street and right on Madison Avenue for some heavenly chocolate ㉑. Take a right on 79th and then a left to stroll along Park Avenue. At 84th Street, turn left back to Madison Avenue for more shopping. Continue to 93rd Street and turn left. At Fifth Avenue, turn left past several of the city's most famous museums ㉒ ㉓ ㉔ ㉕, and keep an eye out for #1040 Fifth Avenue ㉖. The last museum you'll pass is The Metropolitan Museum of Art ㉗. Take a detour to Madison Avenue, between 81st and 80th Street for a little break and snack ㉘. Head back to Fifth Avenue and turn right on 79th Street into Central Park to rent a bike or a boat ㉙, or for a drink and something more to eat ㉚. End the day by checking out the Bethesda Fountain and Terrace ㉛, and then walk over The Mall to the Naumburg Bandshell ㉜.

SIGHTS & ATTRACTIONS

⑤ **The Metropolitan Club** was established in 1891 under the chairmanship of banker J.P. Morgan and inspired by the architecture of Italian *palazzos*. The inside, which is unfortunately only accessible to the private club's members, is extravagantly decorated with Corinthian columns, rich red carpets, marble, and velvet.

1 east 60th street, at 5th avenue, www.metropolitanclubnyc.org, t: (212) 838-7400, not open to the public, n, q & r trains to 5th ave/59th st

⑦ The **Knickerbocker Club,** or "The Knick", as it is informally known, is another of the many private clubs on Fifth Avenue. This gentlemen's club was founded in 1871 by former members of the Union Club, who were concerned that the club's admission standards had fallen. The building dates from 1913 and was designed by the American architects Delano & Aldrich. The building's architecture includes a mix of Georgian and Federal elements.

2 east 62nd street, at 5th avenue, not open to the public, n, q & r trains to 5th ave/59th st

⑧ At 11 East 62nd Street, you'll find the **Edith & Ernesto Fabbri House.** The ornate Neo-Classical mansion with beautiful detailing was constructed in 1916 and is one of the finest examples of Beaux Art architecture in New York City. Edith Shepard Fabbri received this amazing house as a gift from her parents when she married banker Ernesto Fabbri; Edith's mother was a member of the wealthy Vanderbilt family.

11 east 62nd street, between 5th and madison avenue, not open to the public, n, q & r trains to 5th ave/59th st

⑨ **726 Madison Avenue** was built in 1932 for the Bank of Manhattan Company. Although Georgian-style architecture had not been in fashion for nearly a century, the building was designed in this style—as a result, it seems completely out of place on this posh street.

726 madison avenue, at 64th street, not open to the public, 6 train to 68th st/hunter college, f train to lexington ave/63rd st

⑬ The **Roosevelt House** is actually two houses with one shared entrance. Sarah Delano Roosevelt gifted the house to her son Franklin and his new bride, Eleanor, and lived at #47. FDR and his wife lived at #49 while he was recovering from polio in 1921 and 1922. It remained their home base whenever they were in New York. The house was sold following Sarah's death in 1941.

47-49 east 65th street, between madison and park avenue, www.roosevelthouse. hunter.cuny.edu, t: (212) 650-3174, not open to the public, tours by request, set tours sat at 10am, noon & 2pm, 6 train to 68th st/hunter college

⑮ The **7th Regiment Armory,** also known as Park Avenue Armory, seems a bit like a fort. The large brick building was once the headquarters of the seventh regiment of the New York National Guard. The interior is beautifully decorated, but the building itself, which dates from 1880, became dilapidated. In 2006 the Park Armory Conservancy began significant renovations to transform the building into a unique home for unconventional art.

643 park avenue, between 66th and 67th street, www.armoryonpark.org, t: (212) 616-3930, open during exhibitions, see website for exhibition times and prices, tours on request, 6 train to 68th st/hunter college

⑯ The houses on **the west side of Park Avenue, from 68th to 69th Street,** were saved from demolition in 1965 by Marquesa de Cuevas, a member of the wealthy Rockefeller family. She donated the buildings to her favorite charities, including the Americas Society, Spanish Institute, and Istituto Italiano di Cultura. Today you can attend exhibits, readings, and classes here.

park avenue, between 68th and 69th street, 6 train to 68th st/hunter college

⑰ The **Frick Collection** is located in the former home of the Pittsburgh steel magnate Henry Clay Frick, and maintains the same homey feel as when he lived here. The collection includes masterpieces from many famous European artists, such as Van Eyck, Bellini, Titian, and Goya.

1 east 70th street, at 5th avenue, www.frick.org, t: (212) 288-0700, open tue-sat 10am-6pm, sun 11am-5pm, entrance $20, 6 train to 68th st/hunter college

㉒ **The Jewish Museum** opened in 1904 with 26 objects on display. Today the collection includes 26,000 objects that reflect 4,000 years of Jewish art and culture. You'll find everything from archeological artifacts and paintings to videos and interactive websites.

1109 5th avenue, at 92nd street, www.thejewishmuseum.org, t: (212) 423-3200, open mon-tue & fri-sun 11am-5:45pm, thu 11am-8pm, entrance $15, free on saturdays, 6 train to 96th st

㉓ The former home of the famous philanthropist and steel magnate Andrew Carnegie was transformed into the **Cooper Hewitt, Smithsonian Design Museum** in 1977. Visit the museum to see everything from historic to contemporary design, and from one-of-a-kind to mass-produced design objects. The collection includes pieces that are over 2,000 years old.

2 east 91st street, at 5th avenue, www.cooperhewitt.org, t: (212) 849-8400, open sun-fri 10am-6pm, sat 10am-9pm, entrance $16, voluntary donation sat from 6pm, 6 train to 96th st

㉔ The **Guggenheim Museum** is one of the most famous buildings designed by architect Frank Lloyd Wright—the unique architecture is as important as the Picassos and Kandinskys hanging inside. For the ultimate experience, take the elevator to the top and slowly work your way down. Plan to spend at least half a day in the museum. On Saturdays from 5:45pm-7:45pm, you pay what you want.

1071 5th avenue, at 89th street, www.guggenheim.org, t: (212) 759-3000, open sun-wed & fri 10am-5:45pm, sat 10am-7:45pm, entrance $25, 4, 5 & 6 trains to 86th st

㉕ The **Neue Galerie** is devoted to German and Austrian art. The building in which the museum is housed was previously the home of Mrs. Cornelius Vanderbilt, a society doyenne and the widow of one of the richest men in New York. The building also houses two excellent cafés.

1048 5th avenue, at 86th street, www.neuegalerie.org, phone (212) 628-6200, open thurs-mon 11am-6pm, entrance $20, 4, 5 & 6 trains to 86th st/lexington ave, b & c trains to 86th st/central park west

㉖ A year after her husband was assassinated in Dallas, former First Lady Jacqueline Kennedy Onassis moved into the 15th floor at **1040 5th Avenue.** She

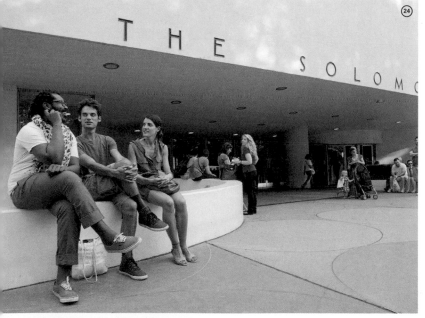

thoroughly valued the anonymity afforded her by people in New York City and often went for walks in Central Park. Jackie lived here until her death in 1994. Two years later, the apartment that she purchased in 1964 for $250,000 sold for $9.5 million, and in 2006 changed hands again for $19.5 million.

1040 5th avenue, not open to the public, 4, 5 & 6 trains to 86th st

㉗ The grand building that houses **The Metropolitan Museum of Art** (the Met) bears a strong resemblance to the Palace of Versailles. In this museum you'll find artwork from ancient and modern times. Various additions have been made to the building over the years, and the Fifth Avenue side dates from 1895-1902. For a nice view, head up to the rooftop garden.

1000 5th avenue, at 82nd street, www.metmuseum.org, t: (212) 570-3828, open sat-thu 10am-5:30pm, fri-sat 10am-9pm, entrance $25 (suggested), 6 train to 77th st, 4, 5 & 6 trains to 86th st

㉛ **Bethesda Terrace** was one of the first structures in Central Park. Its two levels are connected by stately steps. Walk underneath and admire the gorgeous tiled ceiling. At the center of the lower level is **Bethesda Fountain,** the backdrop of many a wedding photo. Brides and grooms come here nearly every day to pose for pictures. This is an especially beautiful spot with a lake, row boats, and grand buildings of western Manhattan in the background.

central park, 72nd street cross drive, www.centralpark.com, open daily 7am-1am, b & c trains to 72nd st, 6 train to 77th st

㉜ The Neo-Classical **Naumburg Bandshell** was built in Central Park in 1923. Since then, artists of all ilks have performed here. Famous people like Martin Luther King, Jr. and John Lennon also stood on this stage. Find out about performances on the Central Park website. **The Mall** runs through the middle of the park, from the Bethesda Terrace down to 66th Street. There are plenty of benches along the Mall, but you may have to compete with the street artists, roller-skaters, and skateboarders to get one.

central park, between east 70th and east 71st street, www.centralpark.com, 6 train to 68th st/hunter college

FOOD & DRINK

③ Behind the brown doors at **The Bar Room** lie an old-style bar and restaurant. A beautiful mural decorates the back room, while a long bar in the front room invites guests to sit and enjoy a cocktail with friends or colleagues. This is a popular spot to stop for drinks on the way home from work. The food here is simple but good—the Bar Room Burger is a favorite.

117 east 60th street, www.thebarroomnyc.com, t: (212) 561-5523, open mon & sun 11am-1am, tue-sat 11am-3am, price $24, n, q & r trains to lexington ave

⑥ Since 1930, **The Pierre** has been one of the most elegant hotels in New York City. Treat yourself to afternoon tea at the Two E lounge here. Or, if you feel like going all out, then opt for their royal tea service, which comes complete with tea, sandwiches, scones, and champagne.

2 east 61st street, www.twoeny.com, t: (212) 838-8000, open daily for afternoon tea 3pm-6pm, price $55, n & r trains to 5th ave/59th st

⑭ Located in the middle of the Upper East Side, **The East Pole** is a popular spot among hip locals. It's the sister restaurant of The Fat Radish (see page 29) on the Lower East Side, so you can expect the same level of quality and service and the same prices at both locations. Vegetable dishes like the roasted parsnips and the walnut and beet hummus are great appetizers. It's an excellent spot for lunch.

133 east 65th street, www.theeastpolenyc.com, t: (212) 249-2222, open mon-fri 11:30am-3pm & 5:30pm-midnight, sat 10:30am-midnight, sun 10:30am-11pm, price $28, f train to lexington ave/63th st

⑳ **Butterfield Express** has been a neighborhood fixture for over a century. Everything at this local market is made fresh, and they have delicious coffee, sandwiches, fruit, and cakes. Buy lunch here, then walk over to Central Park to picnic like the locals do. Don't forget to pick up some homemade frozen yogurt to eat along the way.

1102 lexington avenue, www.butterfieldmarket.com, t: (212) 988-0196, open mon-fri 7am-8pm, sat-sun 8am-5pm, 4, 5 & 6 trains to 86th st

㉘ **E.A.T.** is ideal for a delicious salad or sandwich to refuel after strolling through the streets, shops, and museums along this walk.

1064 madison avenue, between 80th and 81st street, www.elizabar.com, t: (212) 772-0022, open daily 7am-10pm, price $16, 6 train to 77th st, 4, 5 & 6 trains to 86th st

㉚ **The Loeb Boathouse** is a lovely colonial-style restaurant on the water in Central Park. Next to the restaurant, you can enjoy a drink at the Boat Bar and watch as people row past. This is a nice place to end the day

east 72nd street, park drive north, www.thecentralparkboathouse.com, t: (212) 517-2233, open mon-fri noon-4pm, sat-sun 9:30am-4pm (times change during the high and low seasons), price $25, 6 train to 68th st/hunter college

SHOPPING

① Shopping, shopping, shopping is what **Bloomingdale's** is all about. For decades New Yorkers have been coming to this department store's flagship to take advantage of all that the worlds of beauty and fashion have to offer. Curious about what's in all of those Little and Big Brown Bags you see on the street? Head inside to find out. Don't expect to see everything in the store, though—it's huge. Take a good look at the map, because it's easy to get lost in here.

1000 3rd avenue, between 59th street and lexington avenue, www.bloomingdales.com, t: (212) 705-2000, open mon-wed 11am-8:30pm, thu-sat 10am-10pm, sun 10am-9pm, 4, 5, 6, n, q & r trains to 59th st

② You won't want to miss **Sprinkles Cupcake ATM.** Delicious cookies and cupcakes are available 24 hours a day from this cheerfully-colored contraption, a pleasant twist on your average vending machine. All cupcakes are handmade in the shop next door, and the automat is restocked day and night so that it's always filled with freshly baked goodies.

780 lexington avenue, between 60th and 61st street, www.sprinkles.com, t: (212) 207-8375, shop open mon-sat 9am-9pm, sun 10am-8pm, price $4.25, 4, 5, 6, n, q & r trains to 59th st

④ **Barneys** started out selling men's suits and has since grown to become one of the most distinguished stores in all of NYC. Here you'll find designers and brands you won't see in any other department store. Upper East Side moms (or their personal shoppers) come here to buy Dior dresses for their little ones. If you're feeling inspired by the sophisticated style of the locals in this neighborhood, stop by for some additions to your wardrobe—if your credit card limit is high enough.

660 madison avenue, at 60th street, www.barneys.com, t: (718) 388-1655, open mon-fri 10am-9pm, sat 10am-7pm, sun 11am-7pm , n, q & r trains to 5th ave/59th st

⑱ **Christian Louboutin** designs striking shoes recognizable by their iconic red soles. You'll find all of his designs in one place in this store. Unfortunatately, the shoes also come with a hefty price tag.

965 madison avenue, at 74th street, www.christianlouboutin.com, t: (212) 396-1884, open mon-sat 10am-6pm, 6 train to 77th st

㉑ **La Maison du Chocolat** takes chocolate very seriously. Everything you buy from this luxury chocalatier has been imported from Paris. Their exquisite flavors include caviar and vodka, champagne truffles, and chocolates inspired by the popular fragrance *Angel* by Thierry Mugler. Fortunately you can place orders online, because once you've tasted this chocolate, you won't ever want anything else.

1018 madison avenue, between 78th and 79th street, www.lamaisonduchocolat.com, t: (212) 744-7117, open mon-sat 10am-7pm, sun 11am-6pm, 6 train to 77th st

MORE TO EXPLORE

⑩ The **Central Park Zoo** is home to a number of NYC's most beloved inhabitants. The polar bears and sea lions are among the most popular. Come see if any of the main characters from Pixar's *Madagascar* have made it back home yet.

central park, near 64th street at 5th avenue, www.centralparkzoo.com, t: (212) 439-6500, open april-nov mon-fri 10am-5pm, sat-sun 10am-5:30pm, nov-april open daily 10am-4:30pm, entrance $18, n, q & r trains to 5th ave/59th st

⑪ Ice skating at **Wollman Rink** has long been a favorite pastime for many New York City residents. Glide across the ice here from fall through spring. The Victoria Gardens amusement park moves in from July to September.

central park, near 59th street and 6th avenue, www.wollmanskatingrink.com, t: (212) 439-6900, open daily from 10am, entrance mon-thu $11.25, fri-sun $18, skate rental $8, n, q & r trains to 5th ave, a, b, c, d & 1 trains to 59th st/columbus circle

⑫ **Heckscher Ballfields** has six softball and baseball diamonds, and there's nearly always a team practising or a game happening. Sit here and watch a game, and look up from time to time to appreciate the contrast between Central Park and the rest of surrounding Manhattan.

near 63rd street central, www.centralpark.com, open daily 6am-1am, f train to lexington ave/63rd st

⑲ Anyone who thinks cabaret is a thing of the past ought to visit **Café Carlyle** for a dinner show. For years now director Woody Allen has been playing here with his jazz band on Monday nights; if you want to see him it's best to make a dinner reservation. Café Carlyle is located in the Carlyle hotel.

carlyle hotel, 35 east 76th street, at madison avenue, www.thecarlyle.com, t: (212) 744-1600, open mon-sat 6pm-1am, closed july-aug, price $165 for a table, $120 at the bar, exclusive menu, 6 train to 77th st

⑳ Enjoy beautiful Central Park by bike or by boat. Rent a bike or tandem at **Central Park Bicycle Rental,** or rent a boat next door at the **Loeb Boathouse.** Both are available by the hour.

central park, near 74th street, www.thecentralparkboathouse.com, t: (212) 517-2233, open daily april-nov 10am-5pm, price $9-15 per hour, $200 or credit card as deposit, 6 train to 68th st

WALK **5**

UPPER WEST SIDE & HARLEM

ABOUT THE WALK
This long walk, which will take you a good three hours, focuses on African-American culture and historic architecture. The route travels along the Hudson River through picturesque Riverside Park. It's serene in and around the park, and you'll get to see a whole different side of New York City. The last part of the walk will take you through Harlem.

THE NEIGHBORHOODS
Between Central Park and the Hudson River lies the **Upper West Side,** a neighborhood known for its rich intellectual and cultural history. Today it's hard to imagine that, up until the 19th century, this part of New York City was considered the wilderness. The area wasn't built up until after 1880, when construction began on the neighborhood's first apartment complex, **The Dakota.**

With its brownstones and rowhouses, many streets in the neighborhood are considered historic sites. The southern part of the Upper West Side is known as a cultural hub, and in the north, the skyline is dominated by **Riverside Church** and **Columbia University.** In between you'll find a mix of small museums, neighborhood shops, sweet boutiques, and good restaurants.

While Central Park may be the most famous, it's certainly not the only park on the Upper West Side. Along the banks of the Hudson River stretches **Riverside Park.** According to local residents this is Manhattan's most beautiful park, and they come here for sports, leisure, and the cool breeze off the Hudson during the hot city summers.

North of the Upper West Side lies an important center of African-American culture: **Harlem.** Here you'll find art galleries, churches (often named after notable African-American figures), the legendary **Apollo Theater,** and much more. In recent years Harlem has experienced a wave of gentrification, and the neighborhood's historic brownstones and wide streets have been attracting people from around the city.

Upper North Harlem is a bit grittier, so be sure to keep that in mind. The neighborhood is never quiet; people converse loudly in the streets, music can be heard all around, and locals regularly sit on the stoops in front of their homes.

SHORT ON TIME? HERE ARE THE HIGHLIGHTS

**+ THE DAKOTA + COLUMBIA UNIVERSITY + APOLLO THEATER
+ RED ROOSTER HARLEM + RIVERSIDE PARK**

TIPS
// This walk can easily be split in two
// The part of the route along the Hudson is great for biking
// The walk can be done in reverse

UPPER WEST SIDE & HARLEM

1. ABC television studios
2. Columbus Avenue between West 68th & West 72nd Street
3. Malia Mills
4. The Dakota
5. Strawberry Fields
6. Levain Bakery
7. Piccolo Café
8. Aylsmere apartments
9. West 76th Street
10. American Museum of Natural History
11. Zabar's
12. Boat Basin Café
13. Riverside Park
14. Nicolas Roerich Museum
15. Tom's Restaurant
16. General Grant National Memorial
17. Riverside Church
18. Columbia University
19. Alma Mater
20. Low Memorial Library
21. Cathedral of St. John the Divine
22. Hungarian Pastry Shop
23. Morningside Park
24. Apollo Theater
25. Studio Museum
26. Astor Row Café
27. Astor Row
28. Red Rooster Harlem
29. Vinatería
30. Double Dutch Espresso
31. Lido
32. Harlem Tavern
33. Silvana's
34. The Ravine/The Loch

0   250 m

LEGEND

● >> SIGHTS & ATTRACTIONS
● >> FOOD & DRINK
● >> SHOPPING
● >> MORE TO EXPLORE

WALK 5 DESCRIPTION (approx. 9.6 miles)

This route is fairly long, so you may want to split it in two. Stick to the suggested route in Harlem, since not all parts of this neighborhood are as inviting. Begin on the Upper West Side at ABC Television Studios ❶ on Columbus Avenue. Head north and do some boutique shopping ❷ ❸. Then turn left on 72nd Street and walk past the building where John Lennon once lived ❹. Cross the street and head into Central Park. Immediately after you enter, there's a path to Strawberry Fields ❺. Walk back out of the park the way you came in, turning right on Central Park West. Take a left on 74th Street ❻, then a right, and a right again for a bite to eat on 75th Street ❼. Turn left on Columbus Avenue and then right on 76th Street to see some unique buildings ❽ ❾. Continue straight to Central Park West, and then turn left to visit a museum ❿. Head left down 81st Street and left on Broadway for a good deli and some coffee ⓫. Take a right on 80th Street to Riverside Drive and make a left, then at 79th Street make a right into the park. Walk straight to the Boat Basin Café ⓬, then head under the roundabout. Enjoy a drink on the water before walking through Riverside Park, keeping the Hudson River on your left ⓭. Take the tunnel under the road at 83rd Street and continue through the park. Cross 95th Street and continue on the path down to the left and then to the right, heading back into the park. This long walk will take you up along some sports fields. At the last field, walk up and out of the park. Go a short distance down Riverside Drive back in the direction you came from, then turn left on 107th Street for Russian art ⓮. Take a left on Broadway for a famous diner ⓯. Go left on 113th Street, and make a right at the end on Riverside Drive to visit a tomb and a church ⓰ ⓱. Take a right on Claremont Avenue, then a left on 120th Street and a right on Broadway toward the entrance to Columbia University ⓲ ⓳ ⓴. Walk across the campus to Amsterdam Avenue, take a right, and continue straight to see a church and have a drink ㉑ ㉒. Walk back up Amsterdam Avenue and turn right on 113th Street toward Morningside Park ㉓. Walk through the park and then go left on Manhattan Avenue. Turn right on 125th Street to the musical heart of Harlem and take in some culture and art ㉔ ㉕. Head left on Lenox Avenue and then turn right on 130th Street to Astor Row ㉖ ㉗. Turn right and right again, then left back down Lenox Avenue for some soul food ㉘. Take a right on 120th Street and then left on Frederick Douglass Boulevard ㉙ ㉚ ㉛ ㉜ ㉝. If you're up for seeing more nature, continue on to The Lock ㉞.

SIGHTS & ATTRACTIONS

① At **ABC television studios** on the Upper West Side, you can look into the studio from the street during *Good Morning America*. Or maybe you'd like to be part of the studio audience during *Live with Kelly?* Get your tickets in advance online or try your luck in the standby line starting at 7am.

corner of west 67th street and columbus avenue, www.livekelly.com, free, 1 train to 66th st

④ **The Dakota** dates back to 1884. From the outside, it appears to be nothing more than a stately apartment building. Yet people have been flocking to visit this site since December 8, 1980, when John Lennon was shot dead in the street on the way back to his home here. Lennon's wife Yoko Ono still lives in The Dakota today. Other famous (former) residents include Lauren Bacall, Rosie O'Donnell, Bono, Judy Garland, Rudolf Nureyev, Joe Namath, Maury Povich, and Connie Chung. With turrets and spires, the building resembles something of a castle, an intentional design choice to convince wealthy New Yorkers that living in an apartment could be just as luxurious as a house.

1 west 72nd street, not open to the public, b, c, 1, 2 & 3 trains to 72nd st

⑤ Following John Lennon's death, this small spot in Central Park across from The Dakota became a place for people to pay their respects to the inspirational musician. Fans come to **Strawberry Fields** to place flowers on a memorial mosaic bearing the single word "imagine." It's a peaceful place to sit and listen as fans sing and play guitars in tribute.

entrance central park west on west 72nd street, www.centralparknyc.org, t: (212) 310-6600, open daily 6am-1am, b, c, 1, 2 & 3 trains to 72nd st

⑧ The **Aylsmere apartments** are located in a beautiful Renaissance building decorated with brick ornaments. The building dates back to 1894 and was built for the wealthy. Initially there were just two apartments per floor, complete with dining rooms, sitting rooms, bedrooms, bathrooms, and a room for the help. Following the Depression, however, the apartments were split up into smaller units.

331 columbus avenue, not open to the public, 1, 2, 3, b & c trains to 72nd st

⑨ This part of **West 76th Street** gives a good example of the beautiful townhouses and rowhouses so typical of the Upper West Side. They are frequently featured in movies and television series set in New York. Most homes on this street were built between 1887 and 1898.

west 76th street between columbus avenue and central park west, b & c trains to 81st st/museum of natural history

⑩ The **American Museum of Natural History** is one of the biggest museums in the United States and is primarily known for its large collection of dinosaur fossils. The stately museum, which stands across from Central Park, has impressive collections on Native Americans, human biology and evolution, meteorites, minerals, mammals, and much more.

central park west, at west 79th street, www.amnh.org, t: (212) 769-5100, open daily 10am-5:45pm, entrance $22 (or a voluntary donation), b & c trains to 81st st, 1 train to 79th st

⑭ The **Nicolas Roerich Museum** is a small, eccentric museum in a typical Upper West Side townhouse. The Russian artist came to New York City in the 1920s, and this museum displays some 200 pieces of his work. Cards and reproductions of his artwork are available for purchase.

319 west 107th street, www.roerich.org, open tue-fri noon-5pm, sat-sun 2pm-5pm, voluntary donation, 1 train to cathedral pkwy, b & c trains to cathedral pkwy/110th st

⑮ Characters in the popular comedy series Seinfeld regularly ate at the fictional Monk's Café. The inside of the café was a studio, but images of the exterior featured **Tom's Restaurant.** The neon sign above this restaurant is now one of the most recognized in the city. Suzanne Vega's hit song "Tom's Diner" is also based on this spot.

2880 broadway, www.tomsrestaurant.net, t: (212) 864-6137, open sun-wed 6am-1:30am, thu-sat open 24 hours, price $10, 1 train to 110th st

⑯ A popular riddle asks, "Who is buried in Grant's tomb?" The answer, of course, is nobody. The 18th president, General Ulysses S. Grant, and his wife, Julia, were laid to rest at what is now the **General Grant National Memorial.** They are not buried in the tomb, but rather entombed in an atrium above ground.

A Civil War hero, Grant was popular in his time, which explains why his is the second largest mausoleum in North America.

122nd street and riverside drive, www.grantstomb.org, t: (212) 666-1640, open thu-sun 10am-11am, noon-1pm, 2pm-3pm & 4pm-5pm, free entrance, 1 & 9 trains to 116th st

⑰ Standing 392 feet tall, **Riverside Church,** completed in 1930, is the tallest church in the U.S. The building was modeled on the Gothic cathedral of Chartres. Inside the church hangs a carillon with 74 bells—the heaviest in the world. The largest bell weighs 18 tons, and the smallest just 11 pounds.

490 riverside drive, from 120th to 122nd street, www.theriversidechurchny.org, open daily 7am-10pm, free entrance, 1 train to 116th st

⑱ **Columbia University** is one of the oldest, wealthiest, and largest universities in the country, not to mention a prestigious Ivy League school. In 1897, the university moved to its current location in Morningside Heights. The hustle and bustle here, combined with a mix of classic and modern architecture and abundant amounts of green, make this is a truly urban campus. On the impressive list of famous Columbia alumni you'll find the names of figures such as Theodore Roosevelt, John Jay, and Barack Obama.

west 114th to 120th street, from broadway to amsterdam avenue, www.columbia.edu, t: (212) 854-1754, campus open to the public, free entrance, 1 train to 116th st

⑲ The most photographed part of the Columbia University campus is probably the bronze **Alma Mater** statue. With her arms outstretched and an open book on her lap, she appears to be welcoming students and visitors. Hidden somewhere among the folds of her robe is an owl, the symbol of wisdom. Legend has it that the first student of each incoming class to find the owl will graduate at the top of the class.

west 116th street, between broadway and amsterdam avenue, 1 train to 116th st

⑳ **Low Memorial Library** is a classical building dating from 1895. The building, with its dome-shaped roof and row of columns in front, is located in the middle of Columbia University's campus. Despite the name, the building hasn't housed a library since 1934. Instead, it's home to a number of school offices as well as

the Visitors Center (office 213), where you can pick up a campus map. For those interested in the university's rich history, there's a collection of artifacts on display in the building's lobby. When the weather is nice, students often sit on the steps out front.

535 west 116th street, between broadway and amsterdam avenue, t: (212) 854-1754, open mon-fri 9am-5pm, free entrance, 1 train to 116th st

㉑ If bigger is indeed better, then you may never find a better cathedral than that of the **Cathedral of St. John the Divine.** Construction on this colossus, which began in 1891 and is still not complete, has been an immensely time-consuming affair. Every April dozens of cyclists come to the church for the traditional blessing of the bikes. Tours of the cathedral are offered daily.

1047 amsterdam avenue, at 112th street, www.stjohndivine.org, t: (212) 316-7540, open daily 7:30am-6pm, see website for tour times and prices, free entrance, 1 train to 110th st

㉕ The **Studio Museum** was the first in the country dedicated to promoting the work of African-American artists when it opened in 1968. The museum, which feels more like a gallery or studio, displays artwork from the 19th and 20th centuries by African-American artists as well as artists influenced by black culture. In addition to its permanent collection, which contains approximately 2,000 works,.the museum also hosts temporary exhibits, such as historical photos of the Harlem Renaissance in the 1920s.

144 west 125th street, www.studiomuseum.org, t: (212) 864-4500, open thu-fri noon-9pm, sat 10am-6pm, sun noon-6pm, voluntary donation, free on sundays, 2 & 3 trains to 125th st

㉗ **Astor Row** refers to the 28 townhouses on the south side of West 130th Street in Harlem. Designed by Charles Buek and built between 1880 and 1883, the houses were progressive for their time. Each one is three stories, set back about 20 feet from the road, and has a beautiful wooden porch. Many of the original porches have had to be rebuilt.

west 130th street, between 5th and lenox avenue, 2 & 3 trains to 125th st

FOOD & DRINK

⑥ Smell the scent of freshly baked cookies wafting down the street early in the morning. **Levain Bakery** is known for its chocolate chip walnut cookies. The line is often out the door, but the cookies are well worth the wait.

167 west 74th street, www.levainbakery.com, t: (212) 874-6080, open mon-sat 8am-7pm, sun 9am-7pm, price cookie $5, 1, 2 & 3 trains to 72nd st

⑦ **Piccolo Café** is tiny but cozy. This restaurant serves breakfast sandwiches, coffee, and more all day long. This is a good place to come for lunch or at night for dinner. You can also get coffee to go from the window outside.

313 amsterdam avenue, www.piccolocafe.us, t: (212) 873-0962, open mon-fri 8am-11pm, sat-sun 9am-10pm, price $10, 1, 2 & 3 trains to 72nd st

⑫ After walking through Riverside Park, find a table at the **Boat Basin Café** and relax. Drink in hand, you can look out over the marina, the Hudson, and New Jersey as you watch the sun set. This casual outdoor restaurant is open when the weather is nice. The locals especially like to come here in the summer when a cool breeze blows in off the water.

west 79th street near the hudson river, www.boatbasincafe.com, t: (212) 496-5542, open late march-late oct mon-wed noon-11pm, thu-sat noon-11:30pm, sun noon-10pm, price $11, 1 train to 79th st

㉒ In the shadow of the Cathedral of St. John the Divine lies the **Hungarian Pastry Shop.** This spot is so popular among Columbia University students that you'd think it was part of the school's campus. However, other neighborhood residents also like to come here for the delicious selection of pastries and a cup of coffee.

1030 amsterdam avenue, at 111th street, fb: hungarian-pastry-shop-nyc, t: (212) 866-4230, open mon-fri 7:30am-11:30pm, sat 8:30am-11:30pm, sun 8:30am-10:30pm, price coffee $3 (cash only), 1 train to cathedral pkwy (110th st)

㉖ **Astor Row Café** is an informal neighborhood café and a great place to come any time of the day. It is always busy. You'll hear mostly Spanish here, but you'll have no problems ordering in English. The menu features items such as sweet

buns, pancakes, salads, wraps, pitas, homemade hummus, and guacamole. The food is simple and fresh.

404 lenox avenue, fb: astorrowcafe, t: (212) 491-2566, open daily 8am-9pm, price $9, 2 & 3 trains to 125th st

(28) **Red Rooster Harlem** serves up classic soul food: simple but delicious southern fare. The *fried yard bird* is highly recommended. The restaurant is always busy and there's often live music at the bar. If you can't get a table at Red Rooster, you may be able to find a spot at Ginny's Supper Club downstairs.

310 lenox avenue, between 125th and 126th street, www.redroosterharlem.com, t: (212) 792-9001, open mon-thu 11:30am-3pm & 4:30pm-10:30pm, fri 11:30am-3pm & 4:30pm-11:30pm, sat 10am-3pm & 4:30pm-11:30pm, sun 10am-5pm & 4:30pm-10pm, price $27, 2 & 3 trains to 125th st/lenox ave, a, b, c & d trains to 125th st/st nicholas ave

(29) Everything you see in the trendy **Vinatería** restaurant is secondhand and has been repurposed to give it a new life. Delicious cocktails are served at the big

bar, and the food in the restaurant is traditional Spanish-Italian fare made primarily with local, seasonal products.

2211 frederick douglass boulevard, www.vinaterianyc.com, t: (212) 662-8462, open mon 5pm-10pm, tue-thu 5pm-11pm, fri 11am-midnight, sat-sun 11am-10pm, price $22, b, c, 2 & 3 trains to 116th st

(30) A local coffee house in Harlem is something of a rare gem. At **Double Dutch Espresso** you can get a shot of coffee and something yummy to go with it. Sit on the nice patio out back in the summer.

2194 frederick douglass boulevard, www.doubledutchespresso.com, t: (917) 951-9215, open mon-fri 7am-8pm, sat-sun 8am-8pm, price $3, b, c, 2 & 3 trains to 116th st

(31) **Lido** is a favorite Italian restaurant among many downtown New Yorkers. This is mostly thanks to dishes made with organic, seasonal products. The restaurant is set up old-school Italian style and has a nice terrace outside. Renowned chef Serena Bass and owner Susannah welcome you with open arms.

2168 frederick douglass boulevard, www.lidoharlem.com, t: (646) 490-8575, open mon-thu 11:30am-4pm & 5pm-10pm, fri 11:30am-4pm & 5pm-11pm, sat 10:30am-4pm & 5pm-11pm, sun 10:30am-4pm & 5pm-10pm, price $21, b, c, 2 & 3 trains to 116th st

(32) The **Harlem Tavern** restaurant and beer garden is known locally for its live music and DJs. Outside are long picnic tables; squeeze in wherever you can find room. It can get very busy here, especially during big sporting events.

2153 frederick douglass boulevard, www.harlemtavern.com, t: (212) 866-4500, open mon-thu noon-2am, fri noon-4am, sat 11am-4am, sun 11am-2am, price $22, b, c, 2 & 3 trains to 116th st

SHOPPING

(2) **Columbus Avenue between West 68th and West 72nd Street** has a variety of upscale stores worth checking out, if for nothing else than to gawk at the beautiful objects on display.

columbus avenue, between west 68th and west 72nd street, 1 train to 66th st, 1, 2, 3, b & c trains to 72nd st

③ Looking for comfortable, luxury swimwear without frills? Then head to **Malia Mills.** This exclusive Brooklyn brand also sells beautiful summer hats, beach bags, and other accessories, all of which would come in handy for a trip to the Hamptons. Bring a full wallet.

220 columbus avenue, at 70th street, www.maliamills.com, t: (212) 874-7200, open mon-wed & fri-sat 11am-6pm, thu noon-7pm, sun noon-5pm, 1, 2, 3, b & c trains to 72nd st

⑪ The specialty shop **Zabar's,** on Broadway, has been around since 1934. What began as a small shop selling smoked fish has grown into something of an institution. New Yorkers come here for lox, sturgeon, and other Jewish delicacies. The coffee, cheese, oils, and gift baskets are also very popular. Head to the café on 80th Street for coffee and cake.

2245 broadway, at 80th street, www.zabars.com, t: (212) 787-2000, open mon-fri 8am-7:30pm, sat 8am-8pm, sun 9am-6pm, 1 train to 79th st, a, b & c trains to 81st st/museum of natural history

㉝ **Silvana's** is a colorful shop and café in one. The vibe here is a mix of African and Israeli influences, and the store sells a variety of thoughtful objects, from cards and vases to jewelry and handmade clothes. You can also come here for coffee, breakfast, lunch, or dinner, and live music in the bar downstairs.

300 west 116 street, www.silvana-nyc.com, t: (646) 692-4935, open daily 8am-10pm (bar daily 4pm-4am), b & c trains to 116th st

MORE TO EXPLORE

⑬ **Riverside Park** is located on the west side of Manhattan. It stretches about four miles, from 59th Street to 155th Street. This is a good alternative to Central Park if you're seeking someplace green to relax; it's also where residents of the Upper West Side and Harlem go. Go for long walks and bike rides, all while enjoying great views of the Hudson. Near 91st Street is the People's Garden, which is wonderfully maintained by 40 diligent volunteers.

west 91st street, www.nycgovparks.org, t: (212) 496-5542, open from sunrise to sunset, 1, 2 & 3 trains to 96th st

㉓ **Morningside Park** is a beautifully kept oasis of calm—the perfect spot for a break. It's especially appealing in the morning when the sun rises over the hill. Take the stairs down and enjoy excellent views of the park and Harlem. A farmer's market takes place on Saturdays, and there are also regular music performances in the park.

from west 110th to west 123rd street, between manhattan avenue, morningside avenue and morningside drive, www.morningsidepark.org, t: (212) 937-3883, open daily, a & h trains to 116th st

㉔ **Apollo Theater** is where stars are born. Ella Fitzgerald, James Brown, Michael Jackson, D'Angelo, and Lauryn Hill have all performed here. Others have made their debut here during the famous Wednesday night Amateur Night, which is a true one-of-a-kind experience. The theater also has its own Walk of Fame.

253 west 125th street, between adam clayton powell jr boulevard (7th avenue) and frederick douglass boulevard (8th avenue), www.apollotheater.org, t: (212) 531-5300, tickets sold mon-fri 10am-6pm, sat noon-5pm, prices vary, a, b, c, d, 2 & 3 trains to 125th st

㉞ For beautiful, untouched nature, head to **The Ravine** in Central Park. Fallen trees are left where they are so long as they don't block the walking paths, and there are dozens of bird, plant, and flower species you wouldn't expect to find in a place like New York City. **The Loch,** an impressive waterfall, is also located here.

west 110th street, park north between 106th and 102nd street, www.centralparknyc.org, open daily 6am-1am, 6 train to 103rd st

WALK **6**

WILLIAMSBURG

ABOUT THE WALK

This surprising walk to and through Brooklyn's Williamsburg neighborhood is for those who know how to appreciate the good things in life. This walk brings you to countless restaurants, cafés, and vintage stores where New York hipsters eat and shop. The vibe here is creative and dynamic, and the low buildings offer a different view of the city than the skyscraper-filled streets of Manhattan.

THE NEIGHBORHOODS

Until the late 19th century, Williamsburg, **Brooklyn** was primarily a place where the Manhattan elite came for a weekend away. It didn't officially become part of New York City until 1898, when Brooklyn became an NYC borough.

The completion of the **Williamsburg Bridge** in 1903 made it possible for the average person to travel across the East River. Newly arrived immigrants and those escaping the packed tenement buildings of the Lower East Side soon flooded into Brooklyn.

Brooklyn has always been a melting pot of cultures, and this is still evident in Williamsburg. Williamsburg initially sprung up in the area that is now South Williamsburg. Large populations of Hasidic Jews, Puerto Ricans, and Dominicans live in this part of the neighborhood. North Williamsburg, known simply as the "North Side," is home to large Polish and Italian communities.

Recent years have seen more and more young Manhattanites making the move across the water, and Williamsburg has become one of Brooklyn's hippest neighborhoods. While artists and creative types were the trailblazers of this new generation of residents, today there is also a growing influx of young professionals who live and work in luxury apartments on the waterfront, with views of the city. These new buildings are tucked between old, industrial structures such as the

Domino Factory, which you can sail past on the ferry. Restaurants and new secondhand stores open up to cater to the area's new residents all the time.

In creative Williamsburg, street art is a way of life. Nowhere else in New York City will you find so many murals, stickers, and stencils on walls, building facades, lampposts, doors, mailboxes, and curbs. Attentive visitors will notice the recurring work of certain artists throughout the neighborhood. If you haven't been to Williamsburg, you haven't truly seen New York City.

SHORT ON TIME? HERE ARE THE HIGHLIGHTS

**+ MAST BROTHERS CHOCOLATE + MUSIC HALL OF WILLIAMSBURG
+ SMORGASBURG + ARTISTS & FLEAS + FETTE SAU**

TIPS
// Afternoon is a great time to visit Williamsburg
// Come here for happy hour on the weekend
// Williamsburg is easy to reach by ferry, bike, or L-train

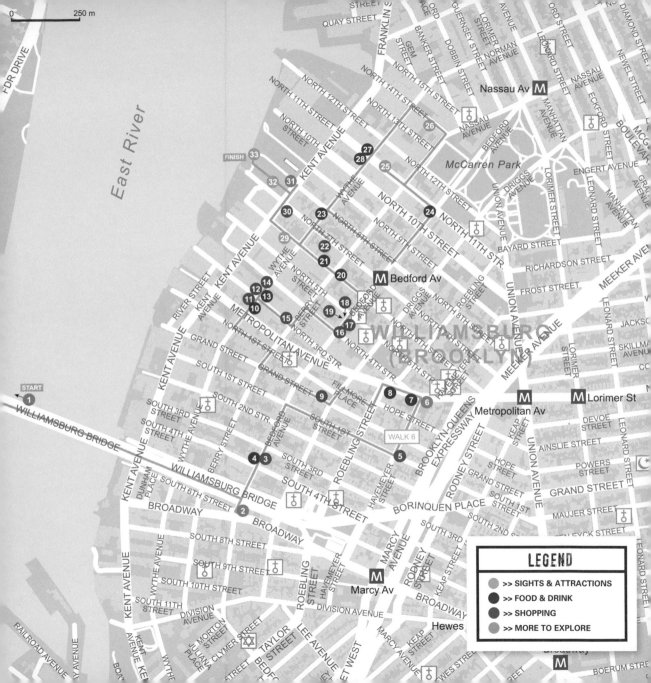

0   250 m

FDR DRIVE

East River

QUAY STREET

FRANKLIN

GUERNSEY STREET
LORIMER STREET
NORMAN AVENUE

Nassau Av [M]

ECKFORD STREET
LEONARD STREET
NASSAU AVENUE
NEWEL STREET

MCG
BOULEVARD

DIAMOND STREET

NORTH 14TH STREET

NORTH 15TH STREET

GEM STREET
BANKER STREET

DOBBIN STREET

NASSAU AVENUE

BEDFORD AVENUE

McCarren Park

ENGERT AVENUE

DRIGGS AVENUE

LORIMER STREET

MANHATTAN AVENUE

GRA
AVENUE

NORTH 13TH STREET
26

FINISH 33

32   31

NORTH 12TH STREET

NORTH 10TH STREET
NORTH 11TH STREET

KENT AVENUE

27
28

25

NORTH 12TH STREET

UNION AVENUE

BAYARD STREET

RICHARDSON STREET
MEEKER AVE

24

NORTH 10TH STR.

NORTH 11TH STR.

ROEBLING STREET

FROST STREET

LEONARD STREET
MANHATTAN AVENUE

30
23

NORTH 9TH STREET

29   WYTHE AVENUE

NORTH 8TH STREET

NORTH 7TH STREET

22

21

20   [M] Bedford Av

NORTH 8TH STREET

DRIGGS AVENUE

BEDFORD AVENUE

NORTH ROEBLING STREET

MEEKER AVENUE

SKILLMAN AVENUE

JACKSON

River STREET

KENT AVENUE

KENT AVENUE

12 14
13
11
10

METROPOLITAN AVENUE

NORTH 1ST STREET

15

WYTHE AVENUE

NORTH 5TH STREET

BERRY STREET

NORTH 3RD STR.

18
19   17
16

WILLIAMSBURG
(BROOKLYN)

NORTH 4TH STR.

NORTH 5TH ST.

UNION AVENUE

LORIMER STREET

GRAND STREET

SOUTH 1ST STREET

GRAND STREET

FILLMORE PLACE

9

HOPE STREET

8
7   6

Metropolitan Av

[M] Lorimer St

START
1

WILLIAMSBURG BRIDGE

GRAND STREET

SOUTH 2ND STR.

SOUTH 1ST STREET

BROOKLYN-QUEENS EXPRESSWAY

RODNEY STREET

DEVOE STREET

AINSLIE STREET

POWERS STREET

GRAND STREET

SOUTH 3RD STREET

BERRY STREET

BEDFORD AVENUE

WALK 6

5

KEAP STREET

HOPE STREET

KENT AVENUE

DUNHAM PLACE
SOUTH 5TH STREET
SOUTH 6TH STREET

WYTHE AVENUE

BERRY STREET

4 3

SOUTH 3RD STREET

SOUTH 4TH STREET

2

BROADWAY

BROADWAY

HAVEMEYER STREET

BORINQUEN PLACE

RODNEY STREET

SOUTH 1ST

SOUTH 2ND

MAUJER STREET

LEONARD STREET

SOUTH 8TH STREET

SOUTH 9TH STREET

SOUTH 10TH STREET

SOUTH 11TH STREET

WYTHE AVENUE

ROEBLING STREET
HAVEMEYER STREET

Marcy Av [M]

MARCY AVENUE

RODNEY STREET

KEAP STREET

SOUTH 3RD

SOUTH 2ND

TEN EYCK STREET

DIVISION AVENUE

KENT AVENUE

MORTON

JULIANA PLACE

CLYMER STREET

TAYLOR STREET

LEE AVENUE

WYTHE

DIVISION AVENUE

BEDFORD

BROADWAY

Hewes

MARCY AVENUE

KEAP STREET

BROADWAY

[M]

BOERUM STRE

RAILROAD AVENUE

KENT KE

BOA

LEGEND

>> SIGHTS & ATTRACTIONS

>> FOOD & DRINK

>> SHOPPING

>> MORE TO EXPLORE

WALK 6 DESCRIPTION (approx. 4.2 miles)

Start in Manhattan and walk across the Williamsburg Bridge ❶, looking back
from time to time to check out the amazing views of the city. Watch out for
bikers. Once on the Williamsburg side, take the ramp down and make a right.
Cross the street and turn left to visit an art gallery ❷. Walk back to where you
came from, go under the bridge, and continue on Bedford Avenue, where you'll
find several shops and places to grab breakfast and coffee ❸ ❹.Turn right on
South 1st Street, which has a stylish shop ❺. Take a left on Havemeyer Street.
To the right on Metropolitan Avenue is a small museum about the city ❻. Walk
back and to the left on Metropolitan Avenue for a barbecue restaurant and the
Roebling Tea Room ❼ ❽. Go left on Roebling Street, right on Fillmore Place, left
on Driggs Avenue, and right on Grand Street for some shopping ❾. Make a right
on Berry Street and then an immediate left on North 1st Street. Then turn right
on Wythe Avenue, where you can munch on some tacos, check out a surf shop,
buy a colorful bag, and do some wine tasting ❿ ⓫ ⓬ ⓭ ⓮. Walk back in the
direction you came from and turn left on North 3rd Street for the famous Mast
Brothers chocolate bars ⓯. Then turn left on Berry Street and take an immediate
right on North 4th Street. Make a left to turn onto Bedford Avenue again, where
you can pick up cheese, jewelry, gadgets, gifts, and vintage clothing ⓰ ⓱ ⓲ ⓳.
Turn left on North 6th Street for a hip coffee house ⓴ and reserve a table for the
evening ㉑. Go right on Wythe Avenue. For a men's clothing and accessories
shop ㉒, take another right on North 7th Street; otherwise, continue straight and
pick up a yummy sandwich at Bakeri ㉓. Take a right further down on North 8th
Street. Turn left on Bedford Avenue and eat in an old garage at The Bedford ㉔.
Turn left on North 11th Street for beer tasting ㉕. Head back to Berry Street and
turn left, then left again on North 14th Street for some bowling ㉖. On Wythe
Avenue take a left and enjoy a drink with a view and a hip design café ㉗ ㉘.
Continue walking to North 6th Street, then turn right for some entertainment ㉙.
Go right on Kent Avenue. On the right at the corner of North 7th Street you'll find
a creative market ㉚. On the other side of Kent Avenue is the East River Park, the
Smorgasburg food trucks, and the ferry back to Manhattan ㉛ ㉜ ㉝.

SIGHTS & ATTRACTIONS

① The **Williamsburg Bridge** connects Manhattan and Williamsburg. It's used by cars and trucks, but you can also cross by bike or on foot. Views of eastern Manhattan from the Williamsburg side are amazing, and since cyclists and pedestrians are separated, getting to the other side is more pleasant and safer than on the Brooklyn Bridge.

corner of delancey street and clinton street, j, m & z trains to essex st, f train to delancey st, b & d trains to grand st

② Kings County Savings Bank previously stood on the spot where the **Williamsburg Art & Historical Center** is now located. This is the best-known gallery in the neighborhood. Exhibits here change regularly and include everything from paintings and sculptures to installations. The center exhibits the work of both American and international artists.

135 broadway, www.wahcenter.net, t: (718) 486-7372, open fri-sun noon-6pm, free entrance, j, m & z trains to marcy ave, l train to bedford

⑥ The tiny **City Reliquary Museum** is definitely not your run-of-the-mill museum. It all started when founder Dave Herman began displaying objects in the windows of his ground-floor Williamsburg apartment. The collection grew as passersby began donating their own quirky items, and in 2006 the museum opened at its current location. It's packed with rare artifacts relating to the history of New York City, including a replica of the Bay Ridge Barbershop—which operated in Brooklyn for 50 years—and a collection of items from the 1964 World's Fair held in New York. The gift shop has fun, interesting items by local artists.

370 metropolitan avenue, www.cityreliquary.org, t: (718) 782-4842, open thu-sun noon-6pm, $5 donation, l train to lorimer st, g train to metropolitan ave

㉛ With its spectacular view looking out over the river onto Manhattan, **East River State Park** is the perfect place to relax and maybe snap a few photos. The park is a great destination for tasty snacks and treats on Saturdays during the Smorgasburg market (see page 137).

3236 north 8th street, www.nysparks.com, open daily 9am-sunset, east river ferry to n 6th st/north williamsburg, l train to bedford ave

FOOD & DRINK

④ Enter the **Rabbithole** and you'll find yourself in a bar/café area where you can get a cup of yummy Stumptown coffee. Order a scone or muffin—baked by Ms. Rabbithole herself—to go with it. The restaurant is to the rear, and the garden out back makes for a fabulous green setting to enjoy a meal.

352 bedford avenue, www.rabbitholerestaurant.com, t: (718) 782-0910, open daily 9am-11pm, price $18, l train to bedford ave, j, m & z trains to marcy ave

⑦ **Fette Sau** is a mandatory destination for all meat lovers. Located in a former garage, the restaurant serves delicious barbecue all year long. Come find a spot at one of the long tables here or, when the weather is nice, enjoy a seat outside. Be sure to get here early, though, or you'll have to wait in line. Your favorite cut of meat may already be gone by the time you get a seat.

354 metropolitan avenue, www.fettesaubbq.com, t: (718) 963-3404, open mon-thu 5pm-11pm, fri-sun noon-11pm, price $18, l train to lorimer st, g train to metropolitan ave

⑧ This building was once a factory. Today it's a charming restaurant with high ceilings, big windows, and flowered wallpaper. And the **Roebling Tea Room** is not just for tea; it also serves lunch and dinner.

143 roebling street, www.roeblingtearoom.com, t: (718) 963-0760, open mon-thu 11:30am-5pm & 6pm-11pm, fri 11:30am-5pm & 6pm-midnight, sat 10am-4:30pm & 6pm-midnight, sun 10am-4:30pm & 6pm-11pm, price $20, l train to bedford ave or lorimer st, g train to metropolitan ave

⑩ **Cafe de la Esquina** is an old-style American diner. Slipping into one of the booths here feels like stepping into an old movie. The restaurant serves up delicious, authentic tacos; tacos al pastor are a favorite with the regulars. DJs often play outside at night, making this diner a popular destination among hip locals.

225 wythe avenue, between metropolitan avenue and north 3rd street, www.esquinabk.com, t: (718) 393-5500, open mon-tue noon-10pm, wed-thu noon-11pm, fri noon-midnight, sat 11am-midnight, sun 11am-10pm, price $14, l train to bedford ave

(13) You don't have to be a wine aficionado to enjoy the delicious local offerings at **Brooklyn Oenology.** They know everything there is to know about wine. Sample a flight of four different wines. Enjoy a snack with your drink, such as a cheese platter or delicious meats including chorizo, prosciutto, and pâté.

209 wythe avenue, www.brooklynoenology.com, t: (718) 599-1259, open mon 4pm-10pm, tue-wed 2pm-10pm, thu 2pm-11pm, fri 2pm-midnight, sat noon-midnight, sun noon-10pm, price wine flight from $15, l train to bedford ave, east river ferry to north 6th st/north williamsburg

(20) **Toby's Estate** is an Australian coffee house. This successful café began years ago in Australia when owner Toby Smith began roasting his own coffee. Years later, the company opened its first American location in Williamsburg. Come here to enjoy delicious coffee in a beautiful space. Their Brew School also offers a variety of classes, including a public cupping class every Saturday afternoon.

125 north 6th street, www.tobysestate.com, t: (347) 457-6160, open mon-fri 7am-7pm, sat-sun 8am-7pm, price espresso $2-$6, price public cupping class $10, l train to bedford ave, east river ferry to north 6th st/north williamsburg

(21) Writers, artists, and other creative souls from the neighborhood like to slide into the old-style booths at **Sweetwater** to enjoy a nice dinner. This American bistro serves up dishes from a variety of areas. On warm summer evenings, the garden is the perfect place to linger until late into the night.

105 north 6th street, www.sweetwaterny.com, t: (718) 963-0608, open mon-fri 11am-midnight, sat-sun 10:30am-midnight, price $20, l train to bedford ave, east river ferry to north 6th st/north williamsburg

(23) **Bakeri** is a small bakery and café with a bohemian vibe. Enjoy freshly baked bread, pastries, and cookies in a charming space full of thoughtful details, such as a collage of picture frames, flowers, and beautiful handwritten cards. The café also serves coffee to go with all its delicious treats. A house favorite is the Norwegian *skolebrød,* a type of sweet bun.

150 wythe avenue, www.bakeribrooklyn.com, t: (718) 388-8037, open mon-fri 7am-7pm, sat-sun 8am-7pm, price $8, l train to bedford ave, east river ferry to north 6th st/north williamsburg

㉔ Located in a former garage, **The Bedford** is a restaurant with a rustic, vintage appearance. The beautiful corner building with a curbside café is a wonderful place for a relaxed night out. Its menu includes classic dishes with a twist, such as the Bedford Plank Burger with garlic aioli and chili ketchup. Already ate? A night at the bar here is a good alternative.

110 bedford avenue, www.thebedfordonbedford.com, t: (718) 302-1002, open mon-thu & sun 11am-11pm, fri-sat 11am-4pm & 6pm-midnight, price $21, l train to bedford ave, east river ferry to north 6th st/north williamsburg

㉗ **Reynard** is trendy bistro inside the gorgeously designed Wythe Hotel. Head upstairs to end the evening with a drink—the fabulous views of the Manhattan skyline are a nice added bonus. DJs regularly play at the rooftop bar and, with a little luck, you might even be able to spot some stars.

80 wythe avenue, www.reynardnyc.com, t: (718) 460-8004, open mon-fri 7am-midnight & 5:30pm, sat-sun 7am-4pm & 5:30pm-midnight, price $26, l train to bedford ave

㉘ Yet another former garage has been reinvented with a new culinary function. In summer the doors to **Kinfolk** stand wide open, giving the wonderful sensation of being outdoors while inside. The centerpiece here is the black walnut bar. The café is open for coffee in the morning, and beer in the evening. Next to the garage is the Kinfolk men's clothing store, which is worth a peek.

90 wythe avenue, www.kinfolklife.com, t: (347) 799-2946, open mon-fri 8:30am-late, sat-sun 11am-late, price $10, l train to bedford ave, east river ferry to north 6th st/north williamsburg

SHOPPING

③ Check out **Fanaberie** for colorful clothes you can be sure no one else back home will be wearing. According to the owner, the items in the store are "eclectic;" we consider them "pleasantly surprising." The fun prints are sure to win you some admiring looks, and the jewelry and bags are all reasonably priced.

339 bedford avenue, www.fanaberienyc.com, t: (347) 335-0252, open mon-sat 10am-8pm, sun 11am-7pm, l train to bedford ave, j, m & z trains to marcy ave

⑤ The owner of **Joinery** is half Brazilian and knows better than anyone where to find beautiful handmade Brazilian blankets and bed linens. She also sells a variety of gorgeous accessories, home decorations, and clothing. Some products are of her own design.
263 south 1st street, www.joinerynyc.com, t: (347) 889-6164, open daily noon-7pm, l train to lorimer st or bedford st

⑨ The owner of **Bird** started out as an assistant buyer for Barneys. Today she has her own stores and sells designer clothes for men and women. This shop also regularly hosts photography and art exhibits.
203 grand street, www.shopbird.com, t: (212) 792-9001, open mon & fri 11am-8pm, tue-thu noon-8pm, sat-sun 11am-7pm, l train to bedford ave

⑪ Surf culture is surprisingly popular in New York City. Come to **Pilgrim Surf** for surf supplies as well as men's street-style clothes, including a great sneaker collection. The shop also sells lifestyle books and accessories. Need to take a minute to digest all the things you've just seen? No problem, just hit up the coffee corner.
68 north 3th street, www.pilgrimsurfsupply.com, t: (718) 218-7456, open daily noon-8pm, l train to bedford ave

⑫ Mociun and Isa Baggu originally opened **Baggu** as a pop-up store, but it was such a success they decided to make it permanent. Their bags are playful, colorful, and minimalist and are available in all sizes and shapes. There's always a place for a Baggu bag in your closet.
242 wythe avenue nr 4, entrance on north 3rd street, www.baggu.com, t: (800) 605-0759, open daily 11am-7pm, l train to bedford ave

⑭ **Mociun** is run by an interior designer, which is immediately visible from the store's wonderfully light space; it looks more like a gallery than a store. Come here for beautiful jewelry, silk textiles, ceramic accessories, and small works of art for special occasions.
224 wythe avenue, www.mociun.com, t: (800) 605-0759, open mon-sun noon-8pm, sun noon-7pm, l train to bedford ave

15

pods
3.
fermentation
3-6 days
4.
SUN
Cacao
Beans are Sun-dried
to Brooklyn
the world
NYC
6.
beans ferment naturally
in wooden boxes & covered
in plantain leaves.
Stone Ground
7.
granite wheels
DR
Roasting
beans are roasted
delicately in ovens.
after shells are
removed, the beans
are ground for 3 days
$7
Single Origin
San Martín
Vanilla
& Smoke
Crown
Maple
Maine
Sea Salt
Cocoa Nibs
Stumptown
Coffee
Serrano
Pepper
MAST BROTHERS CHOCOLATE

⑮ Local chocolatier **Mast Brothers Chocolate** sells beautifully packaged bars of chocolate in flavors such as serrano pepper, Brooklyn blend, and Stumptown coffee. Step inside to smell the delicious aromas and sample one of the many types of chocolate on offer.

111 north 3rd street, www.mastbrothers.com, t: (718) 388-2625, open sat 10am-7pm, sun 10am-5pm, l train to bedford ave, east river ferry to north 6th st/north williamsburg

⑯ The old-fashioned **Bedford Cheese Shop** is a rare gem in New York City and sells cheeses from all around the world.

229 bedford avenue, www.bedfordcheeseshop.com, t: (718) 599-7588, open mon-sat 8am-9pm, sun 8am-8pm, l train to bedford ave, east river ferry to north 6th st/north williamsburg

⑰ **Catbird** is a small store full of old-fashioned toys, cards, knickknacks, and hair accessories. The store's specialty is its great collection of locally-designed jewelry.

219 bedford avenue, www.catbirdnyc.com, t: (917) 599-3457, open mon-sat noon-8pm, sun noon-6pm, l train to bedford ave, east river ferry to north 6th st/north williamsburg

⑱ Hidden in the Mini Mall (to the right of Spoonbill Books) is **MeMe Antenna.** This self-proclaimed gift and music shop is full of cool gadgets and other unique items. You'll find everything from synthesizers, CDs, and LPs to stationery and vintage jewelry.

218 bedford avenue, www.memeantenna.com, t: (347) 223 4219, open daily noon-8pm, l train to bedford ave, east river ferry to north 6th st/north williamsburg

⑲ Audible from all the way down the street, the music at **Awoke Vintage** draws in the neighborhood hipsters. Although alerted to its presence by the music, people come here for secondhand clothes, be it leather jackets, shorts, or fun dresses. With any luck, you'll find that special item you've always been looking for.

132 north 5th street, www.awokevintage.com, t: (718) 387-3130, open daily 10am-9pm, l train to bedford ave, east river ferry to north 6th st/north williamsburg

㉒ **Gentry** is the ideal store for men who are indifferent to shopping. It's a one-stop shop where you can get everything you need to put together a complete outfit. The trendy, high-quality clothes are suitable for the office, and Gentry has a good selection of grooming products on offer as well.

108 north 7th street, www.gentrynyc.com, t: (718) 384-8588, open mon-sat noon-7pm, sun noon-6pm, l train to bedford ave, east river ferry to north 6th st/north williamsburg

㉚ **Artists and Fleas** is open every Saturday and Sunday. Come to this covered market for antiques, vintage items, art, photography, clothes, jewelry, and accessories. Everything is sold by the artists themselves.

70 north 7th street, www.artistsandfleas.com, open sat-sun 10am-7pm, l train to bedford ave, g train to metropolitan ave, east river ferry to north 6th st/north williamsburg

MORE TO EXPLORE

㉕ During the week **Brooklyn Brewery** is only open for tours. But starting Friday afternoon at 5pm, a line forms as people wait for the tasting room to open. The fantastic beers are cheap by NYC standards, and though the brewery doesn't offer much in terms of food, it doesn't mind if patrons get a pizza delivered.

79 north 11th street, www.brooklynbrewery.com, t: (718) 486-7422, open mon-thu 5pm (tours only), fri 6pm-11pm, sat noon-8pm (free tours each hour until 5pm), price beer coins $5, l train to bedford ave, g train to nassau ave, east river ferry to north 6th st/north williamsburg

㉖ People in Williamsburg appreciate a beer and a game of bowling. The neighborhood has three bowling alleys, and **The Gutter** is one of them. Although it opened in 2007, take one step inside and you'll feel transported back to the 1950s. If you have to wait for a lane, pass the time playing an old-fashioned board game.

200 north 14th street, www.thegutterbrooklyn.com, t: (718) 387-3585, open mon-thu 5pm-4am, fri 2pm-4am, sat-sun noon-4am, price from $40/hour, shoe rental $3 (cash only), g train to nassau ave, l train to bedford ave, east river ferry to north 6th st/north williamsburg

㉙ Catch performances by little-known bands every evening at the **Music Hall of Williamsburg.** You'll have a great view of the stage from anywhere in the house, and the acoustics are amazing.

66 north 6th street, www.musichallofwilliamsburg.com, t: (800) 745-3000, williamsburg box office open sat 11am-6pm, manhattan box office (mercury lounge, 6 delancey street) mon-sat noon-7pm, l train to bedford ave, east river ferry to north 6th st/north williamsburg

㉜ Every Saturday some 50 vendors gather at the **Smorgasburg** market to sell homemade snacks and wares. Think hamburgers, sandwiches, ice cream, coffee, tea, and lemonade, as well as clothing and accessories. On Sunday the market moves to Brooklyn Bridge Park Pier 5, and during the winter months it moves inside to 80 North 5th Street all weekend long.

on the east river between north 6th and north 7th street, www.smorgasburg.com, open sat 11am-6pm, east river ferry to north 6th st/north williamsburg

㉝ Instead of heading back to Manhattan on the subway, you can take the **East River Ferry.** Head north and get off at 34th Street, or take a boat south to Pier 11 at Wall Street. New York City is always an impressive sight from the water, and this will soon be an especially pleasant way to reach the neighborhood—the convenient L train between Manhattan and Brooklyn is slated to shut down to undergo repairs for 18 months starting in January 2019.

north 6th street on the waterfront, www.nywaterway.com, open daily, see website for times, price single journey $4, l train to bedford ave

WITH MORE TIME

The walks in this book will take you to most of the city's main highlights. Yet there are still a number of sites worth seeing that are not included in these walks. These are listed below. Note that not all of these places are easily accessible by foot from in town, but you can get to them all using public transportation.

Ⓐ The **United Nations Headquarters** has stood on this spot since 1952. The buildings' simple geometric shapes, glass walls, and lack of cultural references are characteristic of the international style in which it was built. The Visitors Centre is free and regularly hosts interesting exhibits. Guided tours are offered, too.

1st avenue, between 42nd and 48th street, www.un.org, t: (212) 963-8687, open mon-fri 9am-4:30pm (guided tour), sat-sun 10am-4:30pm, entrance $18, s, 4, 5, 6 & 7 trains to grand central/42nd st

Ⓑ The **Brooklyn Museum** is one of the country's oldest and largest museums. Its permanent collection includes a range of objects, including art from various world cultures as well as paintings, sculptures, and more. But it's the museum's temporary exhibitions in particular that draw so many to this stately building, which dates back to 1895. It's impossible to see everything here in one day, so you'll have to make some choices.

200 eastern parkway, www.brooklynmuseum.org, t: (718) 638-5000, open wed & fri-sun 11am-6pm, thu 11am-10pm, 1st saturday of the month 11am-11pm, entrance $16, 2 & 3 trains to eastern pkwy/brooklyn museum

Ⓒ Although officially still in Manhattan, **The Cloisters**—perched on a hilltop above the city—gives the impression you're far away from the urban bustle of NYC. The museum is a branch of The Metropolitan Museum of Art dedicated to medieval art.

99 margaret corbin drive, www.metmuseum.org/visit/visit-the-cloisters, t: (212) 570-3828, open daily march-oct 10am-5:15pm, nov-feb 10am-4:45pm, entrance $25 (tickets can be used the same day at the Met), a train to 190th st, then bus m4 to fort tryon park/the cloisters

Ⓓ **Pieter Claesen Wyckoff House** dates to as far back as 1652, making it the oldest Dutch building in New York City and the surrounding area. The small museum housed here today tells about daily Dutch life in New York centuries ago.
5816 clarendon road, www.wyckoffmuseum.org, t: (718) 629-5400, open fri-sat noon-4pm, entrance $5 (museum visits by tour only), b & q trains to newkirk plaza or 2 & 5 trains to newkirk ave, then bus b8 to beverly rd/ralph ave

Ⓔ Walk along the romantic **Brooklyn Heights Promenade** and take in famous views of the East River, Statue of Liberty, and Brooklyn Bridge. Since the promenade opened in 1950, countless photographers and filmmakers have focused their cameras in this direction by day and by night.
brooklyn heights promenade, entrance from middagh or cranberry street, a & c trains to high st, 2 & 3 trains to clark st

Ⓕ The TV show *Girls* has put the **Greenpoint** neighborhood firmly on the map. The vibe here is laidback, and in recent years many hipsters, musicians, and artists have been drawn to the area thanks to the lower rent. An increasing number of stores, coffee shops, and restaurants continue to move into this incredibly creative neighborhood. Be sure to check out shops like Wolves Within and Line & Label, and don't forget the popular **Homecoming**—a coffee house and flower shop in one.

in the north of brooklyn, on the east river, g train to nassau ave

Ⓖ **DUMBO** (Down Under the Manhattan Bridge Overpass) was once an industrial neighborhood but, while it maintains a bit of a raw edge, has become an increasingly creative and dynamic area. The neighborhood's location on the water at the foot of the Manhattan Bridge give it its unique appearance. Walk through the Brooklyn Bridge Park for great views and then head to Trunk, Mel en Stel, and Powerhouse Books for some good shopping, or go eat oysters at the Atrium. The neighborhood is growing in popularity both among New Yorkers and large companies, such as Etsy, which has set up its headquarters here.

under the manhattan bridge on the brooklyn side, f train to york st

Ⓗ The **Hudson River Park** stretches some 4.5 miles from Battery Park to 57th Street. It's always buzzing and offers lots of activities that won't cost a dime. Come here for kayaking, ice skating, and the playgrounds. There are also tennis courts and boat clubs. A variety of events are organized in the park throughout the year. Tip: There's a scenic two-mile walking route along the Hudson River that starts at Battery Park. Afterward, refresh with a low-key drink at Pier 45. In the summer the grassy field fills up with sunbathers—there are even outdoor showers to help you cool down when it gets too hot.

from battery park to 57th street, www.hudsonriverpark.org, free entrance, 1 train to whitehall st, 5 train to bowling green

Ⓘ The **Museum at FIT** (Fashion Institute of Technology) is a slice of heaven on earth for fashion lovers. It's home to the world's largest collection of garments and accessories, which includes items of fashion and haute couture from the 18th century to the present. There are also regular exhibitions from big names in the fashion world. A visit here is a must during New York Fashion Week. You might even run into a famous designer or blogger.

7th avenue, at w 27th street, www.fitnyc.edu/museum.asp, t: (212) 217-4558, open tue-fri noon-8pm, sat 10am-5pm, free entrance, 1, n & r trains to 28th st

ⓙ New York has a number of great **beaches.** Some are free, while others are not because they have lifeguards. The large Rockaway Beach in Queens is the only beach in New York City where surfing is permitted, and it's accessible by subway and the NYC Beach Bus *(www.nycbeachbus.com).* Long Beach, on Long Island, is about three miles long, and you can walk right out of the train station and onto the sand. Brooklyn's Coney Island—made famous by movies—has a great boardwalk and amusement park, and is easily accessible by subway. Manhattan Beach, also in Brooklyn, is a small family beach just next to Brighton Beach, and people come here for picnics and to barbecue by the water. Beach season in New York officially opens each year on Memorial Day weekend and runs until Labor Day. For more information, visit *www.nycgovparks.org.*

rockaway beach: between beach 9th & beach 149th street, queens, www.nycgovparks .org/parks/rockaway-beach-and-boardwalk, beach open daily 6am-9pm, boardwalk 6am-10pm, free entrance, a train to broad channel, s train to rockaway park–beach 116th st

ⓚ End the day with a stop at the **Upright Citizens Brigade Theatre,** a comedy club for stand-up and improv. Catch shows from the funniest and most creative comedians in the business every evening. Tickets are usually around $10 or less, and shows are free on Sunday nights at 9:30pm.

307 west 26th street, www.ucbtheatre.com, t: (212) 366-9176, open daily, see website for times and shows, price tickets from $5, sun 9:30pm free, 1 train to 28th st, a & c trains to 23rd st

ⓛ **Governors Island** is a small island less than half a mile off the coast of lower Manhattan. For nearly 200 years Governors Island was not accessible to civilians, but it's been open to the public since 2006. Ferries shuttle visitors across the water to this former army base in just seven minutes. Come here for the military history, to check out a festival, to picnic near the Statue of Liberty, or simply to enjoy the greenery and awesome views of the the city's skyline. A good way to explore the island is by bike; bring your own on the ferry or rent one at Bike and Roll when you get here.

governors island, www.govisland.com, open from may 23 to sept 27, mon-fri 10am-6pm, sat-sun 10am-7pm, price ferry ticket $2, 1 train to south ferry, 4 & 5 trains to bowling green, r train to whitehall st

AFTER DARK

New York City and nightlife go hand in hand. Whatever scene you're into—clubs, comedy, jazz, indie music, theater, or film—there's plenty to keep you entertained. NYC doesn't disappoint.

You have to be 21 to get into most bars and clubs. Bring your ID when you go out because you're sure to be carded.

We have all the latest information about nightlife in New York City on our website—from swanky cocktail and wine bars to local pubs and popular clubs. Check out *www.timetomomo.com* and plan your own perfect night out in NYC.

HOTELS

A comfortable bed, tasty breakfast, and inviting interior are all essential ingredients for a pleasant hotel stay. Even more important, however, is location. A hotel is only worth it if you can walk out of the lobby and straight into the bustling city.

New York City has over 100,000 hotel rooms from which to choose. Options include everything from the usual big chains to quaint B&Bs and intimate boutiques to luxury hotels. Airbnb and VRBO offer many options, as well.

If you want easy access to the city's key attractions, then Midtown Manhattan is the place to stay. The modern **Ace Hotel,** for example, is within walking distance of lots of sights. If you're looking for more of a neighborhood feel, **East Village Bed & Coffee** is a popular guesthouse. This small, homey B&B in the hip East Village is close to an array of vintage stores, coffee shops, restaurants, and bars.

WWW.TIMETOMOMO.COM

OUR PERSONAL SELECTION OF HOTELS IN THE HOTTEST NEIGHBORHOODS IN TOWN. GO ONLINE & CLICK TO BOOK.

INDEX

MOON NEW YORK WALKS

FIRST EDITION

Avalon Travel
An imprint of Perseus Books
A Hachette Book Group company
1700 Fourth Street
Berkeley, CA 94710, USA
www.moon.com

ISBN 978-1-63121-600-8

Concept & Original Publication: "time to momo New York" © 2017 by mo'media.
All rights reserved.
For the latest on time to momo walks and recommendations, visit www.timetomomo.com.

MO'MEDIA

TEXT & WALKS
Wendy Mahieu

TRANSLATION
Eileen Holland

MAPS
Van Oort redactie & kartografie

PHOTOGRAPHY
Marjolein den Hartog, René Clement, Wendy Mahieu

DESIGN
Studio 100% & Oranje Vormgevers

PROJECT EDITORS
Heleen Ferdinandusse, Bambi Bogert

AVALON TRAVEL

PROJECT EDITOR
Sierra Machado

COPY EDITOR
Maggie Ryan

PROOFREADER
Megan Mulholland

EDITORIAL INTERN
Rachael Sablik

COVER DESIGN
Derek Thornton, Faceout Studios

Printed in China by RR Donnelley
First U.S. printing, September 2017.

time to momo
MAP APP

Download your free time to momo app from www.timetomomo.com/apps, and know your way around town. For more information, go to:

www.timetomomo.com/mapapp

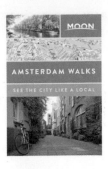

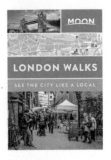
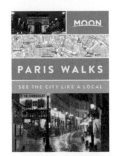
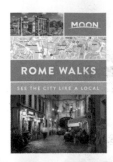